First World War

and Army of Occupation

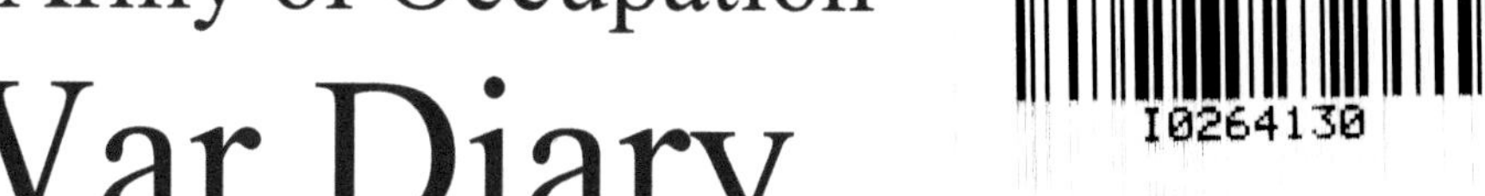

War Diary

France, Belgium and Germany

51 DIVISION
154 Infantry Brigade,
Brigade Machine Gun Company
1 April 1918 - 28 February 1919

WO95/2888/2

The Naval & Military Press Ltd
www.nmarchive.com
Published in association with The National Archives

Published by

The Naval & Military Press Ltd

Unit 10 Ridgewood Industrial Park,

Uckfield, East Sussex,

TN22 5QE England

Tel: +44 (0) 1825 749494

www.naval-military-press.com

www.nmarchive.com

This diary has been reprinted in facsimile from the original. Any imperfections are inevitably reproduced and the quality may fall short of modern type and cartographic standards.

Contents

Document type	Place/Title	Date From	Date To
Heading	51st Division. 154th Infantry Brigade War Diary 1/4th Battalion The Seaforth Highlanders April 1918		
Heading	War Diary of 1/4th Battn. Seaforth Highlanders Volume 43 from 1st April 1918 to 30th April 1918		
War Diary	Busnettes.	01/04/1918	03/04/1918
War Diary	Raimbert	04/04/1918	05/04/1918
War Diary	Ferme du Roi Bethune	08/04/1918	11/04/1918
War Diary	Oblinghem.	13/04/1918	13/04/1918
War Diary	La Miquelerie	14/04/1918	16/04/1918
War Diary	Support Line N.E of Robecq.	17/04/1918	20/04/1918
War Diary	La Brasserie	21/04/1918	22/04/1918
War Diary	Busnes	23/04/1918	24/04/1918
War Diary	St. Hilaire	24/04/1918	30/04/1918
Miscellaneous	1/4th. Battn. Seaforth Highlanders.	16/04/1918	16/04/1918
Map	4th Seaforth		
Miscellaneous	4th. Battn. Seaforth Highlanders.	19/04/1918	19/04/1918
Heading	War Diary of 1/4th Battn Seaforth Highlanders Volume 44 from 1st May 1918 to 31st May 1918		
War Diary	St. Hilaire	01/05/1918	04/05/1918
War Diary	Ecoivres.	05/05/1918	06/05/1918
War Diary	West Camp Roclincourt	07/05/1918	10/05/1918
War Diary	Trenches Right Sub. Sector Oppy Sector	11/05/1918	22/05/1918
War Diary	Ecurie	23/05/1918	28/05/1918
War Diary	Trenches Right Battn. Sub-Sector Gavrelle Sector.	29/05/1918	31/05/1918
Heading	War Diary for June 1918 of 4th Seaforth Vol 33		
Heading	War Diary of 1/4th Battn. Seaforth Highlanders. Volume 45 From 1st June 1918. To 30th June 1918.		
War Diary	Trenches Gavrelle Sector.	01/06/1918	10/06/1918
War Diary	Balmoral Camp Ecurie.	11/06/1918	16/06/1918
War Diary	Trenches Oppy Sector	17/06/1918	28/06/1918
War Diary	Balmoral Camp Ecurie.	29/06/1918	30/06/1918
Operation(al) Order(s)	4th. Bn. Seaforth Highlanders. Operation Order No. 25.	15/06/1918	15/06/1918
Miscellaneous	Appendix "A" Mining Platoon.	15/06/1918	15/06/1918
Operation(al) Order(s)	4th Battalion Seaforth Operation Order No. 27.	27/06/1918	27/06/1918
Heading	154th Brigade 51st (Highland) Division 1/4th Battn. Seaforth Highlanders July. 1918.		
War Diary	Balmoral Camp Ecurie.	01/07/1918	03/07/1918
War Diary	Gavrelle Sector	04/07/1918	11/07/1918
War Diary	Maroeuil.	12/07/1918	12/07/1918
War Diary	Monchy Breton	13/07/1918	16/07/1918
War Diary	Chouilly	16/07/1918	20/07/1918
War Diary	Bois Du Courtron	21/07/1918	27/07/1918
War Diary	Forest Bois Du St. Quentin	27/07/1918	31/07/1918
Heading	War Diary of 1/4th Battn. Seaforth Highrs. (Volume 47) from 1st August 1918 to 31st August 1918		
War Diary	Champillon	01/08/1918	02/08/1918
War Diary	In Train	03/08/1918	03/08/1918
War Diary	Villers Brulin & Bethonsart	04/08/1918	14/08/1918
War Diary	Front Line Trenches Right Sub Sector Gaurelle Sector.	15/08/1918	27/08/1918
War Diary	Dug Outs In Reserve Arras-Bailleul Railway Cutting	28/08/1918	28/08/1918

War Diary	Support Line Nr. Roeux	29/08/1918	31/08/1918
Heading	War Diary of 1/4th Battn. Seaforth Highlanders. (Volume 48) from 1st September 1918 to 30th September 1918		
War Diary	Left Sub Sector Greenland Hill Sector. Front Line	01/09/1918	03/09/1918
War Diary	Wakefield Camp Roclincourt	04/09/1918	10/09/1918
War Diary	Lancaster Camp. Mt St Eloy.	11/09/1918	27/09/1918
War Diary	Left Sub Sector Greenland Hill Sector. Front Line	28/09/1918	30/09/1918
Heading	War Diary of 1/4th Battn. Seaforth Highlanders (Volume 49) From-1st October 1918 To-31st October 1918		
War Diary	In The Line Greenland Hill.	01/10/1918	01/10/1918
War Diary	Mont St Eloy.	02/10/1918	07/10/1918
War Diary	Inchy	08/10/1918	11/10/1918
War Diary	Iwuy.	12/10/1918	14/10/1918
War Diary	Thun St. Martin	15/10/1918	17/10/1918
War Diary	Iwuy	18/10/1918	22/10/1918
War Diary	Douchy	23/10/1918	23/10/1918
War Diary	Denain	24/10/1918	31/10/1918
Miscellaneous	1/4th. Bn. Seaforth Highlanders. History Of Operations from night of 11th. to night of 14/15th. October 1918.		
Miscellaneous	History of Operations by 1/4th Battalion The Seaforth Highlanders 11th-15th October.	18/10/1918	18/10/1918
Miscellaneous	1/4th Bn. Seaforth Highlanders. History of Operations 17/10/18-22/10/18.	26/10/1918	26/10/1918
Miscellaneous	4th. Battn. Seaforth Highlanders.	05/11/1918	05/11/1918
Miscellaneous	Casualties during operations 26th. October to 28th. October 1918.		
Heading	War Diary of 4th Battn. Seaforth Highrs. Volume No. 50. From. 1st November 1918 To-30th November 1918		
War Diary	Fbg. St. Roch	01/11/1918	30/11/1918
Miscellaneous	154th Infantry Brigade.	05/11/1918	05/11/1918
Heading	War Diary of 4th. Battn. Seaforth Highrs Volume 51 from 1st December 1918 to 31st December 1918		
War Diary	Escaudoeuvres	01/12/1918	31/12/1918
Heading	War Diary of 4th Bn. Seaforth Hrs. Vol. 52 from January 1st 1919 to January 31st 1919		
War Diary	St. Roch	01/01/1919	11/01/1919
War Diary	Houdeng Goegnies	12/01/1919	31/01/1919
Heading	War Diary of 1/4th Seaforth Highlanders Vol 53 From 1st Feb 1919 To 28th Feb 1919		
Miscellaneous	Cover for Documents. Nature of Enclosures.		
War Diary	Houdeng-Goegnies	01/02/1919	28/02/1919

51st Division.

154th Infantry Brigade

WAR DIARY

1/4th BATTALION

THE SEAFORTH HIGHLANDERS

APRIL 1 9 1 8

Attached :- Report on Operations 9th-13th April

(Confidential.)

War Diary

of

1/4th Battn. Seaforth Highlanders

Volume 43

from 1st April 1918

to 30th April 1918

Instructions regarding War Diaries and Intelligence Summaries are contained in F. S. Regs., Part II. and the Staff Manual respectively. Title pages will be prepared in manuscript.

WAR DIARY
or
~~INTELLIGENCE SUMMARY.~~
(Erase heading not required.)

Army Form C. 2118.

Place	Date	Hour	Summary of Events and Information	Remarks and references to Appendices
BUSNETTES	1/4/18		Fine weather. Division in Corps Reserve. Reorganising of Companies. Training of Coys in Musketry, P.T & B.T. & Gas drill. Specialist classes in Lewis Gun & Signalling. Captn H.P.T GRAY went to Hospital. A draft of 7 O.R joined the Battn, also 5 Officers - Lieut G.T. GILLIES 2 Lt. J.P. ANDERSON, 2 Lt. A GREEN, 2 Lt AB. MONCUR, 2 Lt, J.D. NIXON.	
	2/4/18		Good day. Training of Coys & Specialists as yesterday. Major J.O. HOPKINSON, D.S.O. M.C 2nd Seaforth Highlanders joined the Battalion from England & took over Command. Lieut A.G. CAMPBELL rejoined the Battn from 154 Trench Mortar Battery.	
	3/4/18		Dull weather. Company drill & training of Specialists as usual	
RAIMBERT.	4/4/18		Battn marched from BUSNETTES to RAIMBERT via LE HAMEL and ALLOUAGNE arriving in billets about 1.30 pm. The Division on arrival in new area became 1st Army Reserve. A draft of 40 O.R joined the Battn.	
	5/4/18		Dull day. Inspection of Companies by C.O. Officers & N.C.Os instructed in Intensive musketry. Lewis Gun practice at range. Baths at Coal mines. Captn H.P.T. GRAY rejoined from Hospital	

Army Form C. 2118.

WAR DIARY
or
INTELLIGENCE SUMMARY.
(*Erase heading not required.*)

Instructions regarding War Diaries and Intelligence Summaries are contained in F. S. Regs., Part II. and the Staff Manual respectively. Title pages will be prepared in manuscript.

Place	Date	Hour	Summary of Events and Information	Remarks and references to Appendices
FERME du ROI BETHUNE	8/4/18		Battn moved off from RAIMBERT at 9 a.m. and marched via AUCHEL - ALLOUAGNE - CHOCQUES and BETHUNE to the FERME du ROI just outside BETHUNE arriving about 1.30 pm ~~A Draft of 40 O.R joined the Battn~~ (Reference Map - LACOUTURE.)	
	9/4/18		Dull misty day. Heavy gun fire heard commencing about 4 a.m. and continuous. The Battn received orders at 1.15 pm from 11th Corps H.Q. to move to LE HAMEL and report to 166 Infy Brigade H.Q., 55th Division. On arrival Companies took up positions in vicinity of LE HAMEL.	
		4.30pm	Orders were received to take up a position S.E of the CANAL de la LAWE, approximately from X 14 a 5.7 to X 8 b. 7. 3. Battalion H.Q were taken up at LE CASAN. On our left we gained touch with the 1/4th South Lancs.	
		7pm	Fresh orders were received to move forward & fill up a gap in the line from LE TOURET on the right to 1/4th South Lancs on the left. Nos. 2 & 3 Companies pushed forward and occupied a line from X 16 c 9.7. to X 15 b. 7 9. Battn H.Q. moved to MESPLAUX FARM and at about 2 30 a.m. again to LES FACONS about X. 15. c 7. 6. Touch on right was gained with 1/5th K.O.R. Lancs and on left with 1/4th SOUTH LANCS. Nos. 1 & 4 Companies took up a line W. of LES FACONS in support running from X 15 c 2.4. to X. 14 b 3.1. A draft arrived at Transport Lines, of 390 O.R and ~~48 O.R. also~~	

A5834 Wt. W4973/M687 750,000 8/16 D. D. & L. Ltd. Forms/C.2118/13.

Instructions regarding War Diaries and Intelligence Summaries are contained in F. S. Regs., Part II. and the Staff Manual respectively. Title pages will be prepared in manuscript.

WAR DIARY
or
~~INTELLIGENCE SUMMARY.~~
(Erase heading not required.)

Army Form C. 2118.

Place	Date	Hour	Summary of Events and Information	Remarks and references to Appendices
	9/4/18		also 2 Officers Captn. C.M. CAMERON and Lieut W. WEIR	
	10/4/18	9 a.m.	On the morning of the 10th the enemy attacked our front at about 9 a.m. He attempted many times to dribble forward and to rush up Machine Guns but was repulsed each time by our fire. The enemy tried on three occasions during the morning to work round both our flanks and was each time repulsed with heavy casualties.	
		1 pm.	At 1 pm the 1/5th. K.O.R Lancs were subjected to an intense bombardment in LE TOURET and later when the enemy attacked they were forced to retire. Immediately news was received of the withdrawal of the 1/5th K.O.R Lancs from LE TOURET, No. 4 Coy were ordered to work up the RUE du BOIS and cover our right flank. No. 1 Company extended to the right and occupied the positions vacated by No. 4 Company. The enemy taking advantage of this retirement tried again on two occasions at 4.30 and 5.15 pm to work round our right flank but was again held in check.	
			At 4.30 pm he also attacked on the left, but after suffering severe casualties from Lewis Gun and rifle fire he returned and abandoned a Machine Gun at X. 16. a 8. 3. On the night of the 10th/11th an inter-Coy relief was carried out and our dispositions, in view of expected enemy movements	

J.O.H.

A5834 Wt. W4973/M687 750,000 8/16 D. D. & I. Ltd. Forms/C.2118/13.

Army Form C. 2118.

Instructions regarding War Diaries and Intelligence Summaries are contained in F. S. Regs., Part II. and the Staff Manual respectively. Title pages will be prepared in manuscript.

WAR DIARY
or
~~INTELLIGENCE SUMMARY.~~
(Erase heading not required.)

Place	Date	Hour	Summary of Events and Information	Remarks and references to Appendices
	10/4/18		and of the withdrawal of the 1/5th K.O.R. Lancs from LE TOURET were slightly readjusted. In the evening a draft of 1 Officer (Captn. C.M. CAMERON) and 118 O.R. arrived at Transport lines.	
	11/4/18		The dispositions of the Battalion at dawn on the 11th were as follows ;-	
			No 4 Coy. X 16 a 3.4 to X. 15. b. 6. 1	
			No 1 " X 15 b. 6. 1 to 1/4th South Lancs	
			No. 3 " 3 platoons from X. 15 d. 2. 4. to X. 15 a. 8. 2, one platoon forming a defensive flank along the RUE du BOIS from X. 15 d. 0. 1. to X. 15. d. 2. 4.	
			No. 2 Coy. From X. 15 c. 5. 9 until in touch with 1/4th South Lancs on left.	
			At 8.30 am the enemy began a heavy bombardment of our positions and at 10 am launched a heavy attack along the whole front. He was checked on our front but made progress on the left. Troops on the left began retiring and parties were seen to surrender. The enemy pushed forward rapidly occupying farm in X. 15 b and making towards LES FACONS imperilling both the left flank and rear of our front companies. Although outflanked and threatened by an encircling movement they held on to their positions and inflicted extremely heavy casualties on the enemy with	

A5834 Wt. W4973/M687 750,000 8/16 D. D. & L. Ltd. Forms/C.2118/13.

Instructions regarding War Diaries and Intelligence Summaries are contained in F. S. Regs., Part II. and the Staff Manual respectively. Title pages will be prepared in manuscript.

WAR DIARY
or
~~INTELLIGENCE SUMMARY.~~
(Erase heading not required.)

Army Form C. 2118.

Place	Date	Hour	Summary of Events and Information	Remarks and references to Appendices
	11/4/18		enfilade fire. At about 2.45 pm the enemy owing to his heavy casualties began to retire, leaving a Machine Gun behind him at X.15.b.1.7. During his retirement the enemy collected in small groups and again he suffered heavy casualties from the Lewis Gun and rifle fire of our forward Companies and the fire of our Artillery all of which were excellent. At about 3 pm a Company of 1st Northumberland Fusiliers moved forward to fill up the gap created by the enemy's advance. Small parties of the enemy who were still holding on or who were lost, retreated and the situation was restored from the Canal de la LAWE to our right. Battn H.Q. moved back about noon to LES GLATIGNIES. The two drafts which arrived on the 9th & 10th inst & were lying at the Transport lines at FERME du ROI, BETHUNE had meantime been divided into 4 Companies. At 1 a.m. on 11th April orders were received by Major M. JOBSON to proceed to the forward area with all available Officers & men. The draft paraded at 2 a.m. and marched off by Coys at 3 a.m., Companies were commanded by the following:– No 1 Coy under Lieut W. WEIR. No 2 Coy " C.S.M. PIERCE No 3 " " Captn. C.M. CAMERON No 4 " " Captn. A. CAMPBELL The four Companies were under the Command of Major M.J. JOBSON.	

Instructions regarding War Diaries and Intelligence Summaries are contained in F. S. Regs., Part II. and the Staff Manual respectively. Title pages will be prepared in manuscript.

WAR DIARY
or
~~INTELLIGENCE SUMMARY.~~
(*Erase heading not required.*)

Army Form C. 2118.

Place	Date	Hour	Summary of Events and Information	Remarks and references to Appendices
	11/4/18		This party marched towards the line for two hours but as the Officers had no maps, references can not be given. They then halted & Major JOBSON went to 154th Infy Brigade H.Q. for instructions. At 6.30 a.m. Nos. 1 & 2 Coys of the draft with Major JOBSON and Lieut. W. WEIR moved away to the left but as both these Officers are now Missing, details of the action of this party are not available but they appear to have been heavily engaged & suffered severe casualties. Nos. 3 & 4 Coys of the draft remained where halted - just to the left of LOCON. The enemy were shelling heavily in this area and the Companies were divided into platoons and spread out over four fields in the vicinity of 154th Infy Brigade H.Q. At 11 a.m. instructions were received for this party to move up in support of the 4th Gordon Hrs. At noon on the 11th this party were holding isolated posts in rear of the 4th Gordons about 600 yards to the left of LOCON. This Company was 131 strong. At 3 pm. the Gordons moved slightly forward and this Coy moved up & occupied posts vacated by Gordons. Half of the Coy were then sent forward to reinforce the Gordons in the front line & remained there for the night.	

A5834 Wt. W4973/M687 750,000 8/16 D. D. & L. Ltd. Forms/C.2118/13.

Instructions regarding War Diaries and Intelligence Summaries are contained in F. S. Regs., Part II. and the Staff Manual respectively. Title pages will be prepared in manuscript.

WAR DIARY
or
~~INTELLIGENCE SUMMARY.~~
(Erase heading not required.)

Army Form C. 2118.

Place	Date	Hour	Summary of Events and Information	Remarks and references to Appendices
OBLINGHEM.	13/4/18		Casualties during operations from 9th – 13th April 1918 (contd.)	
			Other Ranks.	
			Killed in Action 15, Wounded 119, Missing 111, Total 245 O.R.	
LA MIQUELLERIE	14/4/18		Battn moved from OBLINGHEM to billets in LA MIQUELLERIE coming under orders of 154th Infy Brigade and in Brigade Reserve.	
	15/4/18		Dull day. Battn. resting, cleaning up & reorganising.	
	16/4/18		Do Do	
Support line N.E of ROBECQ	17/4/18		Dull day. Battn relieved 7th A. & S. Hrs in support to 61st Division N.E of ROBECQ. Our artillery was active during the evening.	
	18/4/18		Good day. Companies employed strengthening defenses. We had several casualties by artillery fire.	
	19/4/18		Good day. Shelling of back areas by enemy artillery to which ours retaliated.	
	20/4/18		Do. Strengthening of defenses continued. Our aeroplanes were active during the day, one enemy machine being driven down. Our own & enemy artillery active. We had several casualties by shell fire.	

A5834 Wt. W4973/M687 750,000 8/16 D. D. & L. Ltd. Forms/C.2118/13.

JDH.

Instructions regarding War Diaries and Intelligence Summaries are contained in F. S. Regs., Part II. and the Staff Manual respectively. Title pages will be prepared in manuscript.

WAR DIARY
or
~~INTELLIGENCE SUMMARY.~~
(Erase heading not required.)

Army Form C. 2118.

Place	Date	Hour	Summary of Events and Information	Remarks and references to Appendices
LA BRASSERIE	21/4/18		Battn was relieved by 7th A.& S. Hrs. and moved back to reserve line at LA BRASSERIE.	
	22/4/18		Good day. Enemy shelled No 4 Coy with Gas shells.	
BUSNES	23/4/18		Battn was relieved by Royal Berks. During relief the enemy shelled with shrapnel but no casualties. Battn. rested at billets in BUSNES for the night.	
ST. HILAIRE	24/4/18		Battn marched from BUSNES VIA LILLERS to billets in ST. HILAIRE where remainder of 154th Infy. Brigade were billeted. Division in reserve to 11th. Corps	
	25/4/18		Bright day. Major L.D. HENDERSON, one of the original Battn Officers rejoined the Battn from England. Companies cleaning up equipment & clothing. Specialist classes in Musketry & Bombing. Baths at AUCHY-AU-BOIS.	
	26/4/18		Dull day. Companies training in P.T & B.T., Musketry, Saluting & Gas drill. Specialist classes in Bombing, Lewis Gun, Signalling & Sniping under instructors. Musketry practise on rifle range by Nos. 1 & 3 Coys. Baths.	
	27/4/18		Dull day. Usual training programme. Baths. Rifle inspection by Armourer Sergt. Battn concert in Y.M.C.A. hall.	

A5834 Wt. W4973/M687 750,000 8/16 D. D. & L. Ltd. Forms/C.2118/13.

Instructions regarding War Diaries and Intelligence Summaries are contained in F. S. Regs., Part II. and the Staff Manual respectively. Title pages will be prepared in manuscript.

WAR DIARY
or
~~INTELLIGENCE SUMMARY.~~
(Erase heading not required.)

Army Form C. 2118.

Place	Date	Hour	Summary of Events and Information	Remarks and references to Appendices
ST HILAIRE	28/4/18		Dull day. Church Services. Range practise for indifferent shots.	
	29/4/18		Dull weather. Training of Companies & Specialists as usual. The G.O.C 51st Division inspected the Transport.	
	30/4/18		Dull weather. No 2 & 3 Coys training in Company drill, Gas drill, P.T. & B.T. & Musketry. No 4 Coy on rifle range. No 1 Coy at Physical training & Bayonet fighting. Lewis Gun practise on range. Specialist classes in Lewis Gun, Bombing & Signalling under instructor. The Divisional Gas Officer inspected Box Respirators of the Battalion.	

[illegible] Comdg 4th [illegible]

30-4-18

A5834 Wt. W4973/M687 750,000 8/16 D. D. & L. Ltd. Forms/C.2118/13.

1/4th. Battn. SEAFORTH HIGHLANDERS.

===== 0 ===== 0 =====

ACCOUNT OF OPERATIONS from 9th. to 13th. APRIL, 1918.

Reference Map:- LACOUTURE.

9th. The Battalion received orders at 1.15 p.m. from 11th. Corps to move to Le HAMEL and report to 166 Brigade H.Q. On arrival Companies took up positions in vicinity of Le HAMEL. At 4.30 p.m. orders were received to take up a position S.E. of the Canal de la LAWE. Approximately from X.14.a.5.7. to X.8.b.7.3. Battalion H.Q. were taken up at Le CASAN.

On our left we gained touch with the 1/4th. S. Lancs.

At 7.0 p.m. fresh orders were received to move forward and fill up a gap in the line from Le TOURET on the right to 1/4th. South Lancs. on the left. Nos. 2 & 3 Companies pushed forward and occupied a line from X.16.c.9.7. to X.15.b.7.9. Battalion H.Q. moved to MESPLAUX FARM and at about 2.30 a.m. again to Les FACONS about X.15.c.7.6.

Touch on right was gained with 1/5th.K.O.R. Lancs. and on left with 1/4th. South Lancs.

Nos. 1 & 4 Companies took up a line W. of Les FACONS in support running from X.15.c.2.4. to X.14.b.3.1.

10th. On the morning of the 10th. the enemy attacked our front at about 9.0 a.m. He attempted many times to dribble forward and to rush up Machine Guns but was repulsed each time by our fire.

The enemy tried on three occasions during the morning to work round both our flanks and was each time repulsed with heavy casualties.

At 1.0 p.m. the 1/5th. K.O.R. Lancs. were subjected to an intense bombardment in Le TOURET and later when the enemy attacked they were forced to retire.

Immediately news was received of the withdrawal of the 1/5th. K.O.R. Lancs. from Le TOURET, No. 4 Company was ordered to work up the Rue de BOIS and cover our right flank. No. 1 Company extended to the right and occupied the positions vacated by No. 4 Company.

The enemy taking advantage of this retirement tried again on two occasions at 4.30 and 5.15 p.m. to work round our right flank but was again held in check. At 4.30 p.m. he also attacked on the left, but after suffering severe casualties from Lewis Gun and rifle fire he returned and abandoned a Machine Gun at X.16.a.8.3.

On the night of the 10/11th. an inter-Company relief was carried out and our dispositions, in view of expected enemy movements and of the withdrawal of the 1/5th. K.O.R. Lancs. from Le TOURET, were slightly re-adjusted.

11th. The dispositions of the Battalion at dawn on the 11th. were as follows :-

No. 4 Company	X.16.c.3.4. to X.15.b.6.1.
No. 1 "	X.15.b.6.1 to 1/4th. South Lancs.
No. 3 "	3 platoons from X.15.d.2.4. to X.15.a.8.2. One platoon forming a defensive flank along the Rue de BOIS from X.15.d.0.1. to X.15.d.2.4.
No. 2 "	From X.15.c.5.9. until in touch with the 1/4th. South Lancs.

At 8.30 a.m. the enemy began a heavy bombardment of our positions and at 10.0 a.m. launched a heavy attack along the whole front.

11th. contd. He was checked on our front but made progress on the left. Troops on the left began retiring and parties were seen to surrender.

The enemy pushed forward rapidly occupying farm in X.15.b. and making towards Les FACONS imperilling both the left flank and rear of our front Companies. Although outflanked and threatened by an encircling movement they held on to their positions and inflicted extremely heavy casualties on the enemy with enfilade fire.

At about 2.45 p.m. the enemy owing to his heavy casualties began to retire, leaving a Machine Gun behind him at X.15.b.1.7. This was afterwards destroyed by shell fire.

During his retirement the enemy collected in small groups and again he suffered heavy casualties from the Lewis Gun and rifle fire of our forward Companies, and the fire of our artillery all of which were excellent.

At about 3.0 p.m. a Company of 1st.Northumberland Fusiliers moved forward to fill up the gap created by the enemy's advance. Small parties of the enemy who were still holding on or who were lost retreated and the situation was restored from the Canal de la LAWE to our right. Battalion H.Q. moved back about noon to Les GLATIGNIES.

12th. During the night of the 11/12th. the Battalion was relieved by the 1st. NORTHUMBERLAND FUSILIERS and occupied the "G" switch line from X.21.c.5.7. to X.14.d.0.3.

The line was immediately improved and the defence of this position was organised in depth.

13th. On the night of the 12/13th. a belt of single apron wire was erected along practically the whole Battalion front.

On the night of the 13th. the Battalion was relieved by the 1/4th. ROYAL FUSILIERS and proceeded to OBLINGHEM.

Our positions at successive stages of the operations are shown on attached maps.
The comments of the Brigadier of the 166 Brigade and the G.O.C. 55th. Division on work done by this Battalion are attached.

Lieut. Col.
Commanding 1/4th. Bn. Seaforth Highrs.

16th. April, 1918.

1/4th. Battn. SEAFORTH HIGHLANDERS.

ACCOUNT OF OPERATIONS from 9th. to 13th. APRIL, 1918.

Reference Map:- LACOUTURE.

9th. The Battalion received orders at 1.15 p.m. from 11th. Corps to move to Le HAMEL and report to 166 Brigade H.Q. On arrival Companies took up positions in vicinity of Le HAMEL. At 4.30 p.m. orders were received to take up a position S.E. of the Canal de la LAWE. Approximately from X.14.a.5.7. to X.8.b.7.3. Battalion H.Q. were taken up at Le CASAN.

On our left we gained touch with the 1/4th. S. Lancs.

At 7.0 p.m. fresh orders were received to move forward and fill up a gap in the line from Le TOURET on the right to 1/4th. South Lancs. on the left. Nos. 2 & 3 Companies pushed forward and occupied a line from X.16.c.9.7. to X.15.b.7.9. Battalion H.Q. moved to MESPLAUX FARM and at about 2.30 a.m. again to Les FACONS about X.15.c.7.6.

Touch on right was gained with 1/5th.K.O.R. Lancs. and on left with 1/4th. South Lancs.

Nos. 1 & 4 Companies took up a line W. of Les FACONS in support running from X.15.c.2.4. to X.14.b.3.1.

10th. On the morning of the 10th. the enemy attacked our front at about 9.0 a.m. He attempted many times to dribble forward and to rush up Machine Guns but was repulsed each time by our fire.

The enemy tried on three occasions during the morning to work round both our flanks and was each time repulsed with heavy casualties.

At 1.0 p.m. the 1/5th. K.O.R. Lancs. were subjected to an intense bombardment in Le TOURET and later when the enemy attacked they were forced to retire.

Immediately news was received of the withdrawal of the 1/5th. K.O.R. Lancs. from Le TOURET, No. 4 Company was ordered to work up the Rue de BOIS and cover our right flank. No. 1 Company extended to the right and occupied the positions vacated by No. 4 Company.

The enemy taking advantage of this retirement tried again on two occasions at 4.30 and 5.15 p.m. to work round our right flank but was again held in check. At 4.30 p.m. he also attacked on the left, but after suffering severe casualties from Lewis Gun and rifle fire he returned and abandoned a Machine Gun at X.16.a.8.3.

On the night of the 10/11th. an inter-Company relief was carried out and our dispositions, in view of expected enemy movements and of the withdrawal of the 1/5th. K.O.R. Lancs. from Le TOURET, were slightly re-adjusted.

11th. The dispositions of the Battalion at dawn on the 11th. were as follows :-

No. 4 Company	X.16.c.3.4. to X.15.b.6.1.
No. 1 "	X.15.b.6.1 to 1/4th. South Lancs.
No. 3 "	3 platoons from X.15.d.2.4. to X.15.a.8.2. One platoon forming a defensive flank along the Rue de BOIS from X.15.d.0.1. to X.15.d.2.4.
No. 2 "	From X.15.c.5.9. until in touch with the 1/4th. South Lancs. on left

At 8.30 a.m. the enemy began a heavy bombardment of our positions and at 10.0 a.m. launched a heavy attack along the whole front.

11th. contd. He was checked on our front but made progress on the left. Troops on the left began retiring and parties were seen to surrender.

The enemy pushed forward rapidly occupying farm in X.15.b. and making towards Les FACONS imperilling both the left flank and rear of our front Companies. Although outflanked and threatened by an encircling movement they held on to their positions and inflicted extremely heavy casualties on the enemy with enfilade fire.

At about 2.45 p.m. the enemy owing to his heavy casualties began to retire, leaving a Machine Gun behind him at X.15.b.1.7. This was afterwards destroyed by shell fire.

During his retirement the enemy collected in small groups and again he suffered heavy casualties from the Lewis Gun and rifle fire of our forward Companies, and the fire of our artillery all of which were excellent.

At about 3.0 p.m. a Company of 1st.Northumberland Fusiliers moved forward to fill up the gap created by the enemy's advance. Small parties of the enemy who were still holding on or who were lost retreated and the situation was restored from the Canal de la LAWE to our right. Battalion H.Q. moved back about noon to Les GLATIGNIES.

12th. During the night of the 11/12th. the Battalion was relieved by the 1st. NORTHUMBERLAND FUSILIERS and occupied the "G" switch line from ~~X.21.d.0.4.~~ X 21 c 5 7 to X.14.d.0.3.

The line was immediately improved and the defence of this position was organised in depth.

13th. On the night of the 12/13th. a belt of single apron wire was erected along practically the whole Battalion front.

On the night of the 13th. the Battalion was relieved by the 1/4th. ROYAL FUSILIERS and proceeded to OBLINGHEM.

~~Our positions at successive stages of the operations are shown on attached maps.~~
~~The comments of the Brigadier of the 166 Brigade and the G.O.C. 55th. Division on work done by this Battalion are attached.~~

J.H. Tomkinson

Lieut. Col.
Commanding 1/4th. Bn. Seaforth Highrs.

16th. April, 1918.

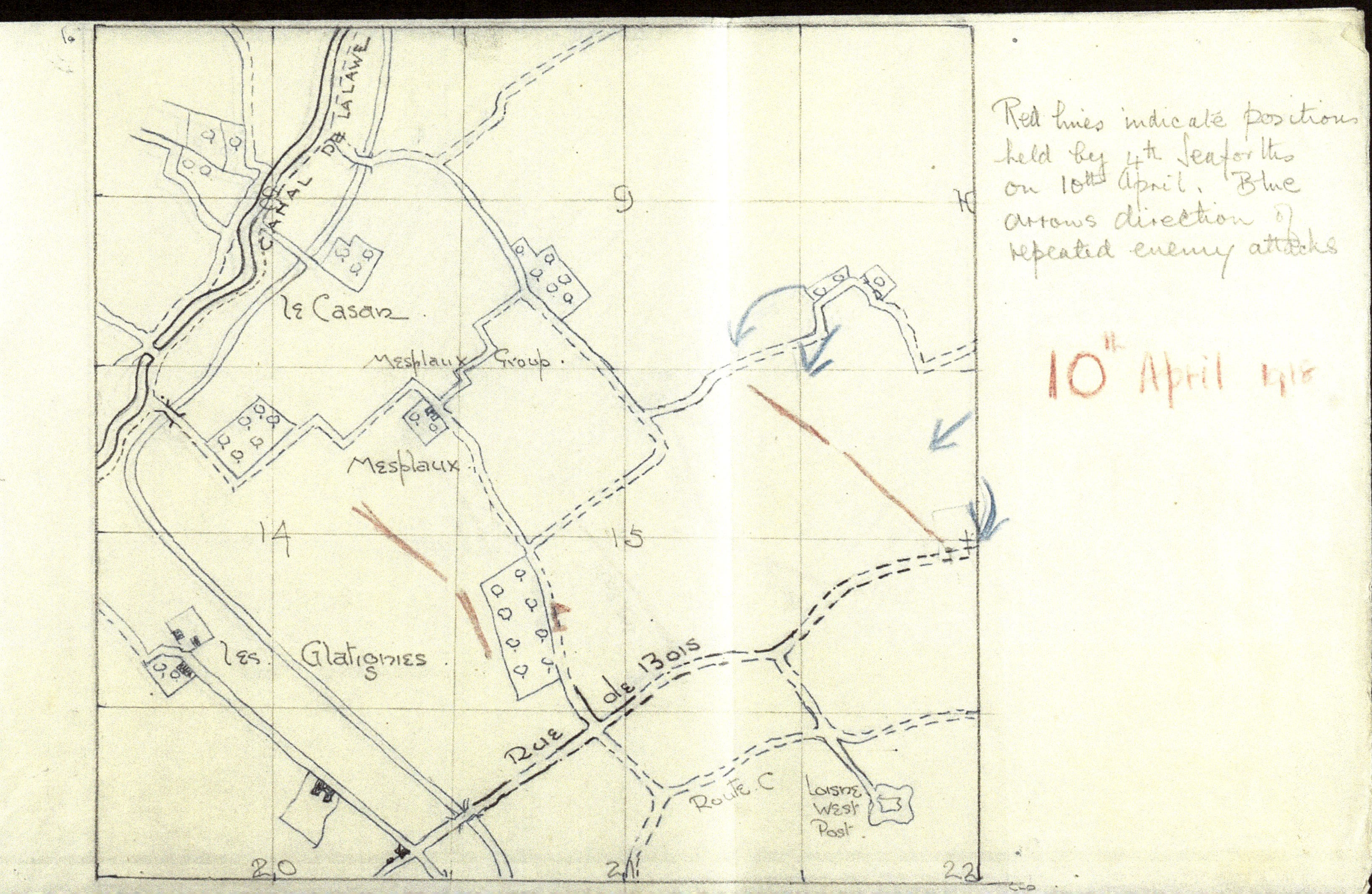

Red lines indicate positions held by 4th Seaforths on 10th April. Blue arrows direction of repeated enemy attacks
10th April 1918
CANAL DE LA LAWE
le Casan
Mesplaux Group
Mesplaux
Les Glatignies
Rue de Bois
Route C
Loisne West Post
9
10
14
15
20
21
22
4th Seaforths

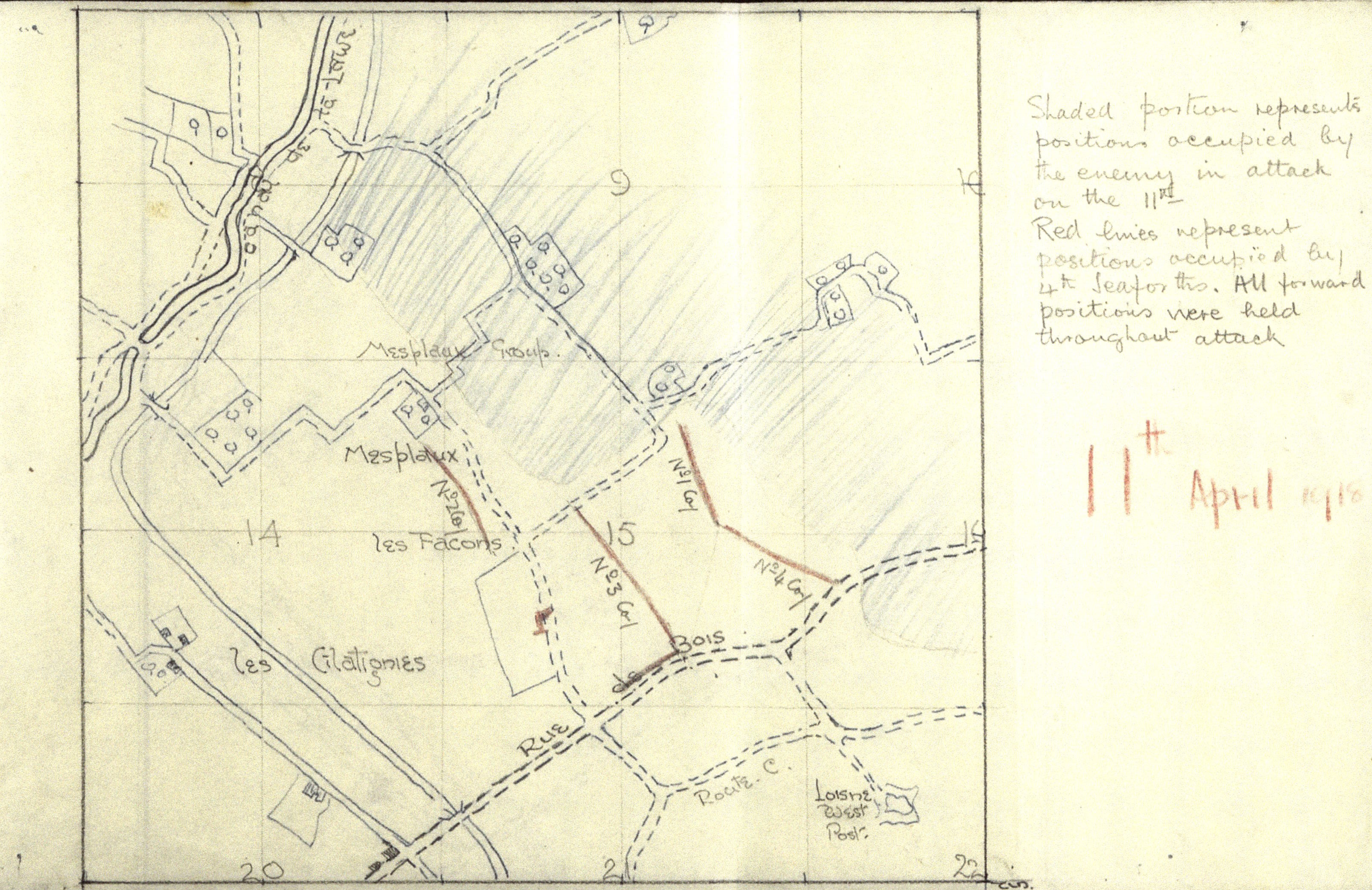
Canal de la Lawe
Mesplaux Group.
Mesplaux
Les Facons
No 1 Coy
No 2 Coy
No 3 Coy
No 4 Coy
Les Glatignies
Bois
Rue
Route C.
Loisne West Post.
9
14
15
16
20
21
22
cms.
Shaded portion represents positions occupied by the enemy in attack on the 11th
Red lines represent positions occupied by 4th Seaforths. All forward positions were held throughout attack
11th April 1918
4th Seaforths

Canal de la Lawe
le Casan
Mesplaux Group
Mesplaux
Les Facons
Les Glatignies
Rue de Bois
Route C
Loisne West Post
9
14
15
20
21

Red line and small circles represent line and shell hole positions taken up by 4th Seaforths on relief. Dotted red line represents approximate front line on 12th

12th April 1916

4th Seaforths

4th. Battn. SEAFORTH HIGHLANDERS.

Defence Scheme - ROBECQ Sector.

The Sector. The village of ROBECQ is a long straggling village with numerous small farms. There are a number of small ditches in and around the village and many hedges affording good cover from view.

The main approaches to the village and the village itself are held by three Companies (two in front and one in support) and Battalion H.Q. The right sector and approaches are held by one Company which also acts as a reserve Company to the Battalion. mobile reserve

two platoons of

The main entrances to the village itself afford many excellent covered approaches to the enemy and it is from this direction that a hostile attack is to be expected.

On the right of the village there is a wide stretch of flat open country in front of our defences and an attack from this direction should be easily repulsed.

General Principles.

The village is to be held at all costs and every man is to have this explained to him. Each Company will detail a small force (to be held in reserve), for the purpose of launching immediate local counter-attacks in the event of the enemy penetrating any portion of the defences.

The defence should as far as possible be organised in posts with an all-round field of fire. Owing to the nature of the country it is impossible to dig trenches deeper than from 18" to 2'. Posts should be banked up and great care should be taken to make them bullet-proof. Positions for snipers will be found in farm-houses commanding likely approaches.

Organisation of Defences.

The following sectors in th e defences are allottedto the various Companies:-

Right Front Company:- The right front Company is responsible for the approaches to the village in Q.19.c., P.24.d. and P.30.b.

Left Front Company:- The left front Company is responsible for the defences of the main road leading into the village and will be disposed as on attached disposition map.

Right Reserve Company:- Is responsible for holding defences of roads leading into village in P.30.a. & c. The right of this Company extends to P.30.c.20.75. road exclusive. This Company has a post also in the centre of the village at P.29.b.7.9. For dispositions see attached map.

Left Support Company:- Is responsible for holding the defences in the village along the main road in square P.24.c. and P.23.d. See attached map.

Action in the event of attack. All Companies take up their battle position at the first indication of a hostile attack. The right reserve Company moves forward 4 Sectionsto occupy 2 Posts in each of the two lines in P.30.b.

Battalion H.Q. Battalion H.Q. is at P.23.c.00.35.

Aid Post. Is at P.23.d.65.35.

Liaison. Liaison will be maintained with units in front and units on flanks. Liaison should also be maintained between M.G.C. and T.M.B. and R.E. who have orders with regard to demolition of bridges.

Wire. The wire is at present mostly capable of great improvement and every effort should be made to thicken belts already in existence and to wire between trees and in suitable hedges. Existing wire is shown on attached map. There are knife rests in readiness to be placed across the main road and special parties should be detailed for this duty.

Ammunition. The minimum ammunition supply should be at the rate of 4 Boxes per Platoon (to be kept with each Platoon in the line) and 8 Boxes at Company H.Q.

Thirty-six boxes should be kept at Battalion H.Q.

<u>Emergency Posts</u>. In the event of the troops in front retiring they should be (according to circumstances) either sent back or retained to help in the defence of the village.
Suitable emergency posts should be prepared and special parties detailed to stop any further withdrawal.

<u>Communication</u>. All Companies are connected to Battalion H.Q. by telephone. When runners are employed they should be warned not to use main roads but the overland track shown on attached map.

<u>Anti-Aircraft</u>. No opportunity will be missed for engaging low flying hostile aeroplanes with Lewis Gun and rifle fire Each Company should have one Lewis Gun detailed for A.A. defence.

<u>Bridges</u> Bridges are shown on attached maps. Arrangements should be made to burn small wooden bridges in event of withdrawal. Arrangements should also be made with R.E. with regard to demolishing larger bridges.

Lieut. Col.
Commanding 1/4th.Bn.Seaforth Highlanders.

19th. April, 1918.

(Confidential)

War Diary

of

1/4th Battn. Seaforth Highlanders.

Volume 44

from 1st. May 1918.

to 31st. May 1918.

Army Form C. 2118.

Instructions regarding War Diaries and Intelligence Summaries are contained in F. S. Regs., Part II. and the Staff Manual respectively. Title pages will be prepared in manuscript.

WAR DIARY
or
~~INTELLIGENCE SUMMARY.~~
(Erase heading not required.)

Place	Date	Hour	Summary of Events and Information	Remarks and references to Appendices
ST. HILAIRE	1/5/18		51st (H) Division in reserve to XIth Corps. Dull day. Training of Coys in Gas drill musketry, P.T. & B.T. Musketry practise on rifle range. Specialist classes in Lewis Gun, Signalling, Bombing, Scouting. The C.O. inspected No 4 Coy. JOR	
	2/5/18		Bright day. Battn carried out practise attack. Specialist classes as usual. Brigade Musketry competition held. Battn Sports in the afternoon. JOR	
	3/5/18		Bright day. Training of Coys in drill, Musketry, P.T. & B.T. Usual specialist classes. No 4 Coy on rifle range. Inspection of Nos 1 & 2 Coys by C.O. 7 new Officers joined the Battn:- Lieut T.F. SCOTT, Lieuts A.A. FINNIGAN, 2 Lieuts W.D. ARMSTRONG, F.S. CLARK, M.C. ELLIS, H.B. LAWSON, P. GRAY. JOR	
	4/5/18		The Transport moved by road to DIVION. Training of Coys as usual. No 3 Coy on rifle range. C.O. inspected H.Q. Coy. Specialists as usual. JOR	
ECOIVRES	5/5/18		Wet day. Battn marched off from ST HILAIRE at 7 am & entrained at LILLERS about 11 a.m., arrived at MAROEUIL Station 3.30 pm & marched to YORK HUTS at ECOIVRES. JOR	
	6/5/18		Dull day. Training of Coys & Specialists. JOR	
WEST CAMP ROCLINCOURT	7/5/18		Wet day. Battn marched from huts at ECOIVRES to WEST Camp, ROCLINCOURT arriving about 1 pm. JOR	

A5834 Wt. W4973/M687 750,000 8/16 D. D. & L. Ltd. Forms/C.2118/13.

Instructions regarding War Diaries and Intelligence Summaries are contained in F. S. Regs., Part II. and the Staff Manual respectively. Title pages will be prepared in manuscript.

WAR DIARY
or
~~INTELLIGENCE SUMMARY.~~
(*Erase heading not required.*)

Army Form C. 2118.

Place	Date	Hour	Summary of Events and Information	Remarks and references to Appendices
WEST CAMP ROCLINCOURT.	8/5/18		Bright day Coys carried out 2 hours training. Specialist classes as usual. JOH. C.O. & Coy Commanders reconnoitred the line. 3 platoons of the Battn relieved posts occupied by 4th Gordon Hrs. JOH	
	9/5/18		Bright day Training of Coys. & Specialists as usual. JOH.	
	10/5/18		Cold day Baths at ROCLINCOURT. Party of 4 Officers & 400 O.R. supplied digging cable trench for Divisional Signals. JOH.	
TRENCHES RIGHT SUB-SECTOR OPPY SECTOR	11/5/18		Cold day Battn relieved 7th Black Watch in right front sub-sector of OPPY SECTOR. 7th Argylls on left, 152 Inf Bde on right. Nos. 2 & 3 Coys in front line, Nos 3 & 4 Coys in Support. JOH	
	12/5/18		Bright day. Coys employed in cleaning trenches & surroundings. Quiet. JOH	
	13/5/18		Do. Strengthening defences etc Do. JOH.	
	14/5/18		Do. Coys making new bays & repairing trenches. Enemy shelled right Support Coy. JOH	
	15/5/18		Bright day & very warm. Work on trenches continued. Aircraft active on both sides. A few heavies landed near Battn H.Q. JOH.	

A5834 Wt. W4973/M687 750,000 8/16 D. D. & L. Ltd. Forms/C.2118/13.

Army Form C. 2118.

WAR DIARY
or
~~INTELLIGENCE SUMMARY~~.
(Erase heading not required.)

Instructions regarding War Diaries and Intelligence Summaries are contained in F. S. Regs., Part II. and the Staff Manual respectively. Title pages will be prepared in manuscript.

Place	Date	Hour	Summary of Events and Information	Remarks and references to Appendices
TRENCHES RIGHT SUB-SECTOR OPPY SECTOR	16/5/18		Bright day. Quiet on our front. Enemy shelled sector on left with gas shells. Vicinity of Battn H.Q. shelled with heavies. [illegible]	
	17/5/18		Very warm day. Working parties supplied to R.E.s cleaning old dugouts Support Coys bathed. A few heavies landed near Battn H.Q. [illegible]	
	18/5/18		Fine day. Work on trenches continued. Enemy shelled vicinity of Battn H.Q. causing some casualties to 7th. Argylls. [illegible]	
	19/5/18		Very warm day. Artillery very quiet. Aircraft active on both sides. Usual working parties supplied. [illegible]	
	20/5/18		Bright day. Enemy sent about 50 shells near Battn H.Q. [illegible]	
	21/5/18		Dull day. Our aeroplanes & artillery very active. A German walked across to our lines & gave himself up. [illegible]	
	22/5/18		Dull windy day. During the night & early morning our artillery bombarded enemy trenches. At night our own & enemy aeroplanes were very active. [illegible]	
ECURIE	23/5/18		Very dull day & strong wind. Battn was relieved by 6th. Seaforth Highrs 152 Inf Brigade & moved back to huts in ECURIE. 154th Inf. Bde in Divisional Reserve. [illegible]	

Army Form C. 2118.

Instructions regarding War Diaries and Intelligence Summaries are contained in F. S. Regs., Part II. and the Staff Manual respectively. Title pages will be prepared in manuscript.

WAR DIARY
or
~~INTELLIGENCE SUMMARY.~~
(Erase heading not required.)

Place	Date	Hour	Summary of Events and Information	Remarks and references to Appendices
ECURIE	24/5/18		Dull wet day. Cleaning up & resting. JOH	
	25/5/18		Bright day. Inspection of Companies by C.O. JOH	
	26/5/18		Dull day. Sunday. Church Parades. JOH	
	27/5/18		Bright day. Training of Coys & Specialists. Rifle inspection by Armourer Sergeant. JOH	
	28/5/18		Bright day. Good observation. Enemy shelled camp & vicinity intermittently during the day, but no casualties to this Battn. An Enemy aeroplane flew over camp very low about 5 pm & was engaged by Lewis Guns & Anti aircraft but escaped. Companies at musketry practise on range at BRAY. JOH	
TRENCHES RIGHT BATTN. SUB-SECTOR GAVRELLE SECTOR	29/5/18		Bright day. Battn relieved 6th Black Watch, 153 Inf Brigade in Right Bn. Sub-sector, GAVRELLE Sector. 15th Division on right. 4th Gordons on left. No 3 Coy in right front, No 2 Coy left front, No 4 Coy reserve, No 1 Coy, Post Line. Relief completed in daylight. No casualties. JOH	
	30/5/18		Fine day. Intermittent shelling on both sides. Party supplied for work under R.Es on new front line was shelled on way up. 3 O.R. Killed & 6 O.R. Wounded. JOH	
	31/5/18		Warm day. Usual working parties. Artillery fairly active on both sides. JOH	

J O H Hopkinson .... LIEUT. COLONEL
COMDG. 1/4th BN. SEAFORTH HIGHRS

A5834 Wt. W4973/M687 750,000 8/16 D. D. & L. Ltd. Forms/C.2118/13.

(6339) Wt. W160/M3016 1,500,000 10/17 McA & W Ltd (E 1898) Forms W3091. Army Form W.3091.

Cover for Documents.

Nature of Enclosures.

War Diary
for
JUNE 1918.
of
4th Seaforth Hrs

Notes, or Letters written.

Confidential.

WAR DIARY

of

1/4th Battn. Seaforth. Highlanders.

Volume 45.

From 1st June 1918.

To 30th June 1918.

Army Form C. 2118.

WAR DIARY
or
~~INTELLIGENCE SUMMARY.~~
(Erase heading not required.)

Instructions regarding War Diaries and Intelligence Summaries are contained in F. S. Regs., Part II. and the Staff Manual respectively. Title pages will be prepared in manuscript.

Place	Date	Hour	Summary of Events and Information	Remarks and references to Appendices
TRENCHES GAVRELLE Sector.	1/6/18		Battalion in Bde. Reserve. Warm weather. Observation good and many Balloons up. Enemy shelled Railway Cutting and POINT DU JOUR REDOUBT. Coys. employed making new front line. JH.	
	2/6/18.		Fine day. Divisional front re-organized – two battalions in front – one in reserve – ~~Our~~ Battn. in reserve. Working parties found for R.E. JH.	
	3/6/18		Fine day. During the night enemy artillery active. Usual working parties supplied. JH.	
	4/6/18.		Bright day. Artillery normal. Aircraft very busy patrolling the whole day. JH.	
	5/6/18.		Fine day. Aerial activity on both sides normal. Enemy shelled our cookhouse killing one man and wounding another. Our artillery carried out harassing fire. JH.	
	6/6/18.		Warm day. Aircraft and artillery as usual. Many balloons up, observation being excellent. We sent out a Patrol which reconnoitred THAMES ALLEY up to the enemy's wire. JH.	
	7/6/18.		Dull morning but brightened up during the day. A Patrol was again sent and gained some useful information regarding the enemy's positions. The enemy raided the Battalion on right but was unsuccessful. JH.	
	8/6/18.		Warm day. Working parties found for R.E. Our artillery shelled enemy's wire. Patrol was sent out with the object of raiding enemy post if opportunity offered but found enemy on the alert and returned – no casualties. JH.	
	9/6/18.		Dull day with fresh wind. Argyll Patrol took prisoner affording normal identification. Gas was successfully discharged on our front. A draft of 42 O.R. joined Battalion. JH.	

A5834 Wt. W4973/M687 750,000 8/16 D. D. & L. Ltd. Forms/C.2118/13.

Instructions regarding War Diaries and Intelligence Summaries are contained in F. S. Regs., Part II. and the Staff Manual respectively. Title pages will be prepared in manuscript.

WAR DIARY
or
~~INTELLIGENCE SUMMARY.~~
(Erase heading not required.)

Army Form C. 2118.

Place	Date	Hour	Summary of Events and Information	Remarks and references to Appendices
TRENCHES GAVRELLE Sector	10/6/18		Bright day. Our aircraft busy all day. Artillery normal. Battalion was relieved by the 5th Bn. Seaforth Hrs. and marched back to huts at Balmoral Camp ECURIE. Relief in daylight and no casualties. JOB	
BALMORAL CAMP ECURIE.	11/6/18.		Dull windy day. Companies cleaning up, reorganizing and resting. Three new Officers joined Battn. — Lieut. F. McCallion M.C., 2/Lts. J Wood and R. Thomson. JOB	
	12/6/18		Dull day. Companies inspected by the Commanding Officer. One hours training in Musketry and Platoon drill carried out. Baths at ROCLINCOURT. Whole Battalion on Working Party under 400 Field Coy. R. E. JOB	
	13/6/18.		Bright day. The Commanding Officer distributed Congratulatory Cards for gallantry. Training in Musketry, Platoon and Gas Drill and P. T. & B. T. JOB	
	14/6/18		Dull day. The XVII Corps Commander presented Medal Ribbons to 154 Infantry Brigade. Work on Camp and training for Divisional Sports. JOB	
	16/6/18.		Dull day. Companies firing on the Range. Musketry & P. T. for one hour. Training for Divisional Sports. JOB	
	16/6/18.		Fine day. Battalion relieved the 7th Bn. Black Watch by daylight in the OPPY Sector. We had no casualties. Spoiling parties for new dugouts supplied. Artillery on both sides normal. Considerable aerial activity. JOB	

A5834 Wt. W4973/M687 750,000 8/16 D. D. & L. Ltd. Forms/C.2118/13.

Army Form C. 2118.

WAR DIARY
or
INTELLIGENCE ~~SUMMARY~~.
(*Erase heading not required.*)

Instructions regarding War Diaries and Intelligence Summaries are contained in F. S. Regs., Part II. and the Staff Manual respectively. Title pages will be prepared in manuscript.

Place	Date	Hour	Summary of Events and Information	Remarks and references to Appendices
TRENCHES OPPY Section	17/6/18.		Fine day. Slight increase in artillery on both sides. Our aircraft busy. Working parties supplied for R.E. JOH	
	18/6/18.		Excellent weather. Artillery normal. Our aircraft kept enemy guns busy all day. During the night our patrols were busy but no identifications procured. Enemy trench mortar shelled part of Front Coy. killing 1 Off. & 5 O.R. – 2/Lt. F. Gray. JOH	
	19/6/18.		Dull and slight rain. Companies employed cleaning up trenches and strengthening defences. Artillery on both sides quiet. JOH	
	20/6/18.		Dull day. Nothing of importance. Usual working parties. JOH	
	21/6/18		Do. Much aerial activity. Artillery on both sides quiet. JOH	
	22/6/18		Do. Usual working parties. Do. Inter-Company relief. No casualties. JOH	
	23/6/18		Wet day. Coys. employed relaying trenchboards and cleaning trenches. Usual R.E. working parties supplied. Artillery quiet. JOH	
	24/6/18		Dull and cold day. Usual working parties. During night companies employed on wiring and strengthening existing wire. Our artillery carried out a destructive shoot. Our aeroplanes active. JOH	
	25/6/18		Fine day. Aircraft busy. Heavy bombardment during the forenoon on the front of Division on our right. Companies strengthening defences. JOH	

A5834 Wt. W4973/M687 750,000 8/16 D. D. & L. Ltd. Forms/C.2118/13.

Instructions regarding War Diaries and Intelligence Summaries are contained in F. S. Regs., Part II. and the Staff Manual respectively. Title pages will be prepared in manuscript.

WAR DIARY
or
~~INTELLIGENCE SUMMARY~~.

(Erase heading not required.)

Army Form C. 2118.

Place	Date	Hour	Summary of Events and Information	Remarks and references to Appendices
TRENCHES OPPY-Sector.	26/6/18.		Fine day. Aircraft on both sides exceptionally busy. Three men wounded by shrapnel from aircraft shelling. Destructive shoot carried out by our artillery on enemy's wire. J.D.H.	
	27/6/18.		Fine day. Much aerial activity. Artillery very busy all day. Companies wiring and constructing and reconstructing fire bays on new system. J.D.H.	
	28/6/18.		Fine day. Our aircraft busy. Artillery normal. Battalion relieved by the 5th. Bn. Seaforth Hrs. and march back to huts in Balmoral Camp ECURIE. Relief carried out in daylight – no casualties. J.D.H.	
BALMORAL Camp ECURIE.	29/6/18		Fine day. During the night and early morning artillery on both sides exceptionally busy. Enemy aircraft over camp in the early morning. Companies reorganising and cleaning up. J.D.H.	
	30/6/18		Bright day – fresh wind. Our artillery very busy all night and early morning. Church Parade and baths. Camp inspected by Commanding Officer. J.D.H.	

J. D. Hopkinson Lieut. Colonel,
Commanding 4th Bn Seaforth Hrs.

A5834 Wt. W4973/M687 750,000 8/16 D. D. & L. Ltd. Forms/C.2118/13.

4th. Bn.Seaforth Highlanders.

OPERATION ORDER No. 25.

Reference Map
MAROEUIL 1/20,000.   15th. June 1918.

1. RELIEF. The Batt alion will relieve the 7th.Black Watch in the Right sub sector of the OPPY SECTOR on the 16th June .
The po sit ion of Companies on relief will be as follows:-
Fr o nt Coys. .... No.4 Coy. on right - No. 1 Coy. on left.
Post Line .... No. 3 Coy.
Reserve .... No. 2 Coy.

2. ORDER OF MARCH. No.4 - 1 - 3 - 2 Coys. & H.Q. Coy. Platoons at 300 yards interval. Route. 400 yards N. and parallell to CONCRETE ROAD. - Duck board track - OUSE ALLEY .
NOTE. TOMMY ALLEY will not be used W. of Post Trench
ZERNER ALLEY will NOT be used.
DRESS. Fighting kit. Overcoats. Waterbottles filled. Leading Coy. will march off at 12.45 p.m.

3. GUIDES. Guides at the rate of 1 per platoon , 1 per Coy. H.Q., 1for Bat tn. H.Q. and 1 for Aid Post will be met at 2.15 p.m. at junctian of OUSE ALLEY and BRIERLY HILL (B.20.b.1.8.) at 2.15 p.m.

4. BATTALION H .Q. will be at B.21.a.8.3.

5. LEWIS GUNS. will be loaded on limbers by 12.15 p.m. Limbers will move off with leading platoons of each Coy. Guns will be collected at B.19.c.5 .5. One man per gun will accompany limbers.

6. SURPLUS MESS KITS AND VALISES. Surplus Mess Kits will be stacked in shed opposite Ord rly Room at 12.30 p.m. and valises at 10.45 a.m. Mess Ki t s and Dixies for the line will be in shed opposite Orderly Room aft er Batt alion moves off. 1 Cook per Coy. & 1 mess servant per Coy . will be left in charge of above.

7. PACKS. wi ll be ~~loaded~~ dumped in shed opposite Orderly Room by 10.45 a.m.

8. ADVANCE PARTY An advance party of the following will report at H.Q. of 7t h. Black Wat ch at 10.0 a.m. :-
2Lieu t. Clark and Sergt. Macdonald for Battn.H.Q.
On e Officer per Company and 1 N.C.O. per Platoon.
Company and Battalion Gas N.C.Os.
First shifts of mining platoons. The above will take over all tren ch stores , gas applainces and reserve rations and will make themeselves thoroughly acquainted with their Sectors and will remain in the line. . The party will parade outside Orderly Room un der 2/Lieut.Clark at 8.30 a.m.
Adv nce party will proceed by same route as Battalion.

9. ECHELON "B " will remain behind in BALMORAL Camp to clean up and will then proceed under 2/Lieut.Green to ECOIVRES to accomodation vacat ed by 153rd.Infantry Brigade.

10. PETROL TINS. 16 Petrol tins will be issued to each of front line Coys.

11. All maps , phot os , schemes of work , defence schemes and trench stores wi ll be taken over on relief . Receipted lists will be sent t oBatt n .H.Q. by 9 a.m. on 17th. inst.

12. Disposit ion maps showing posts and location of platoons will be for warded to Battn. H.Q. by 9 a.m. on 18th. inst.

13. Brigade H.Q. will close at A.20 d.3.2. at 6 p.m. and open at B.14.a.6 .1. at 7 p.m. on 16th. June.

14. Completio n of relief will be reported to Battn.H.Q. by Code phrase "Your S.D.100 received".

15. 2/Lieut . Green will hand over Camp Stores to representative of ~~7th Black Wat ch~~ relieving unit and will obtain receipts for all Camp stores and cert ifi cates of cleanliness which will be handed in to Orderly Room . Li st of Camp Stores can be obtained from Orderly Room.

(Sgd.)W.Surrey Dane
Captn., Adjt.

APPENDIX "A"

MINING PLATOON.

No. 3 Comp any will provide the following Mining platoon for work as under :-

1. DUGOU T. "ADDICKS" B. 22.b.1.6.

2. Worki ng under 404 Field Coy. R.E.

3. Miner s detailed by Field Coy .

4. Spoilers detailed by No. 3 Coy.

5. Size of Shifts - 1 N.C.O. and 12 O.R.

6. Hours of relief - 4 p.m. - 12 midnight - 8 a.m.

The first shifts of the above Party will proceed to the line with the advance par ty at 8.30 a.m. tomorrow and will take over work at 2 p.m. The Officer who proceeds in advance from No. 3 Coy. will take over above work and see that first shift reports to time. and wor k is started. Rations are being sent up early for this party.

Wi th regard to Mining shifts it must be clearly understood that shi fts must be kept up to strength. An Officer will be in charg e of the work and if any man becomes a casualty he must be r eplaced. All reliefs for shifts will report 10 minutes before t i me.

(Sgd.) W. Surrey Dane,
Captn., Adjt.

15/6/ 18.

SECRET

4th Battalion Seaforth [illegible]

Operation Order No. 27.

Reference Map:-
MAROEUIL Sheet, 1/20,000 — 27th June 1918

1. Relief. The Battalion will be relieved by the 5th Sea[illegible] H[illegible] tomorrow, June, 28th, 1918, and on relief will proceed to [illegible] Camp, ÉCURIE.

No. 1 Coy. 4th Seaforths will be relieved by "B" Coy, 5th Seaforths
2 " " " " " "C" Coy. do.
3 " " " " " "A" Coy. do.
4 " " " " " "D" Coy. do.

2. Guides. Guides will be supplied as per relief table attached. Each guide will be given a chit stating the Coy. he belongs to and which Coy. he is guiding and [illegible] of his Platoon. Lt. Dickson will act as O.C. Guides, [illegible] and all guides will report at Battn. H.Q. at 9.30 am. tomorrow. [illegible] will be taken by Lt. Dickson to reconnoitre rendezvous at B.20.b.1.8. On return from reconnoitring one guide per Coy. will remain at Battn. H.Q. to guide advance parties of incoming unit to their respective Coy. All guides will report outside Battn. H.Q. again at 1.30 pm. They will then be taken by Lt. Dickson to rendezvous. Lt. Dickson will be responsible that all guides reach rendezvous to time.

3. Advance Parties. The usual advance parties of incoming [illegible] will report at Battn. H.Q. at 10 am. tomorrow. These parties will [illegible] first shifts of "Spoilers" working on the following dugouts:-

No. 1. - No. 4 Company H.Q.
2. - ADDICKS.
3. - B.23.a.0.9

4. All air photos, schemes of work, trench stores and anti-gas appliances will be handed over on relief. Receipted lists of trench stores will be obtained; also certificates of sanitation & cleanliness which will be handed into Orderly Room by 10.0 am. on the 29th. All petrol tins and [illegible] food containers will be handed over to relieving unit, whose attention should be specially drawn to the extra water tins which are [illegible] held in case of emergency.

5. Lewis Guns. Lewis Guns will be loaded on limbers at B.[illegible] on CONCRETE ROAD. One man per gun will accompany limbers. Mess Kits and tins will be loaded at same place.

6. No party larger than the equivalent of a Platoon will move together. Platoons will move at 300 yards distance. Coy. Commanders will issue strict instructions in order to ensure that servants, cooks, runners, etc. do not straggle down independently.

7. Work on dugouts will be handed over to the [illegible] units at the following times.

1. B.17.c.25.20. - 5th Seaforths - 5.0 pm.
2. ADDICKS. - do. - do.
3. TED TOMMY. - 6th do. - do.
4. B.23.a.0.9. - 5th. do. - do.

Coy. Commanders will arrange for an Officer to take first shifts of relieving unit to work and to explain all details of work on hand. They will also arrange for shifts working on dugouts at time of relief to come [illegible] under an Officer, should the Coy. have been relieved.

154th Brigade

51st (Highland) Division

1/4th Battn. SEAFORTH HIGHLANDERS

JULY, 1918.

Instructions regarding War Diaries and Intelligence Summaries are contained in F. S. Regs., Part II. and the Staff Manual respectively. Title Pages will be prepared in manuscript.

WAR DIARY
or
~~INTELLIGENCE SUMMARY~~
(Erase heading not required.)

Army Form C. 2118.

July, 1918.

4th Battn. Seaforth Highlanders.

Place	Date 1918	Hour	Summary of Events and Information	Remarks and references to Appendices
Balmoral Camp ECURIE.	July 1st.		Brigade in Divisional Reserve. Fine day. Enemy shelled St. NICHOLAS and ARRAS-LENS RD with H.V's. Coy. training in camp.	J.O.W.
	2nd.		Dull day. Companies practicing for proposed raid. Battn. scheme carried out at night.	J.O.W.
	3rd.		Bright day and warm. 2 Platoons No. 1 Coy. and No. 4 Coy. practice for raid. Remainder of Battn. carry out usual training around camp. Practice for Divisional Sports.	J.O.W.
GAVRELLE Sector	4th.		Misty day. The Battn. less raiding party relieved the 1/6th Black Watch in the GAVRELLE Sector by daylight. No casualties. Bn. in Brigade reserve.	J.O.W.
	5th.		Fine day. Lt. Col. Hopkinson took over command of Brigade, Major Henderson assuming command of Battn. Raid cancelled and party joined Battn in the line. Large working parties for new trench supplied.	J.O.W.
	6th.		Dull day. Enemy strafed Railway Cutting with heavies & shrapnel. Usual working parties supplied.	J.O.W.
	7th.		Fine day. Enemy again shelled Railway Cutting. Suspected spy at No. 2 Company H. Qrs. turned out to be a Labour Coy. Officer. Usual working parties supplied.	J.O.W.

2449 Wt. W14957/M90 750,000 1/16 J.B.C. & A. Forms/C.2118/12.

Army Form C. 2118.

WAR DIARY
or
~~INTELLIGENCE SUMMARY~~.

(Erase heading not required.)

Instructions regarding War Diaries and Intelligence Summaries are contained in F. S. Regs., Part II. and the Staff Manual respectively. Title pages will be prepared in manuscript.

Place	Date	Hour	Summary of Events and Information	Remarks and references to Appendices
GAVRELLE Sector	1918 July 8th		Fine day but dull. On the Right Divisional Front an intense barrage (ours) opened at 9.30 pm. Usual working parties supplied.	
	9th		Fine day. In early morning the 152 Bde. raided enemy lines but did not secure identification. Enemy plane was brought down by one of our aircraft about Bde. HQrs.	
	10th		Fine day. Abnormal train movement behind enemy lines. Usual working parties supplied.	
	11th		Fine day but dull. Battn. relieved by 54th Bn. Canadian Infy. by daylight. No casualties. March back to billets in MARDEUIL.	
MARDEUIL.	12th		Showery and mild. Battn: cleaning up. Entrain at ANZIN at 6. pm. for MONCHY. BRETON.	
MONCHY BRETON	13th		Raining. Bn. in billets cleaning up. Kit inspection. 21 O.R. joined Battn.	
	14th		Raining. Early in morning enemy planes over. Battn. entrained at BRYAS for unknown destination. Lt. C. M. McEwing and 17 OR. joined Battn.	
	15th		Bright day. In train.	
	16th		Dull day. Arrived early in morning at NOGENT. Proceed by motor convoy under order of French Military Authority (5th Army) to neighbourhood of CHOUILLY where we debussed about 2 pm. Spent afternoon in wood close by. Received orders in evening to billet in CHOUILLY but found billets insufficient,	

A5834 Wt. W4973/M687 750,000 8/16 D. D. & L. Ltd. Forms/C.2118/13.

Army Form C. 2118.

WAR DIARY
or
~~INTELLIGENCE SUMMARY.~~
(Erase heading not required.)

Instructions regarding War Diaries and Intelligence Summaries are contained in F. S. Regs., Part II. and the Staff Manual respectively. Title pages will be prepared in manuscript.

Place	Date 1918	Hour	Summary of Events and Information	Remarks and references to Appendices
CHOUILLY	July 16th		Bivouaced in open under ½ hours notice. Transport proceeded by road to AVISE. Bombed during night. 8 wounded.	
	17th		Close sultry day till night when heavy thunder storm and rain. Battn. at 1 hours notice. Ready to support 131 French Cal. Div. counter attacking at 11 am. Remained in Bivouacs during day.	
	18th		Heavy rain during early morning. Cleared up to fine & cool weather. Moved from river to wood 1 mile away at 5 pm.	
	19th		Fallen out at 4 am. and proceeded by road to clearing in Wood North of CHAMPHILLON. Fine weather & very warm. Proceeded to line in evening and heavily shelled on way up. 1 Killed. 1 Wounded & 1 accd.	
	20th		Fine morning. The Battn. attacked enemy lines. On right 62nd Division; 153rd Bde. on left. Captured 72 prisoners including 2 Officers. Our casualties heavy. Held up on our Right owing to the 62nd Div. having to retire, on our left owing to French giving wrong jumping-off point but made good progress in spite of both these obstacles. Line runs through BULLIN. Disposition of Companies - Right No. 1. Centre - No. 2. Left No. 4. Support No. 3. Major Henderson from surplus personnel to command 4th Gordons. Line runs O. 1. 6. 6 - BULLIN - 8. 0. 35. 35.	

A5834 Wt. W4973/M687 750,000 8/16 D. D. & L. Ltd. Forms/C.2118/13.

Instructions regarding War Diaries and Intelligence Summaries are contained in F. S. Regs., Part II. and the Staff Manual respectively. Title Pages will be prepared in manuscript.

Army Form C. 2118.

WAR DIARY
or
INTELLIGENCE SUMMARY
(Erase heading not required.)

Place	Date 1918	Hour	Summary of Events and Information	Remarks and references to Appendices
BOIS DU COURTON	July 21st		Dull day. 152 & 153 Brigades attacked enemy on our left but made very little progress.	
	22nd		Bright day. Usual intense shelling by both sides but nothing of importance to report.	
	23rd		The Corps launched an attack this morning. Our Battn. in support to division. Good barrage but too short on left. Casualties slight. About 30 prisoners passed through our hands.	
	24th		During early morning Battn. H.Qrs. shifted but ran shelter & passed out of new position and returned to the old place. Incessant shelling by both sides all day.	
	25th		During night 24/25th we relieved the 4th Gordons in the line. On way up Battn. H.Qrs. was caught in barrage which was put up by mistake. No casualties. Quiet day and clear.	
	26th		Dull day and raining. All morning and forenoon we were subjected to intense shellfire. We were relieved by 6th Black Watch and marched back to BOIS DE ST QUENTIN where Battn. bivouaced for night. Shelled on way out whilst passing through NANTEUIL LA FOSSE.	
	27th		Dull day and raining. Battn. in bivouac in FOREST BOIS DU ST QUENTIN. Men busy cleaning and drying. Bn. under ½ hours notice.	

2449 Wt. W14957/M90 750,000 1/16 J.B.C. & A. Forms/C.2118/12.

Army Form C. 2118.

Instructions regarding War Diaries and Intelligence Summaries are contained in F. S. Regs., Part II. and the Staff Manual respectively. Title pages will be prepared in manuscript.

WAR DIARY
or
~~INTELLIGENCE SUMMARY.~~
(Erase heading not required.)

Place	Date 1918	Hour	Summary of Events and Information	Remarks and references to Appendices
Forest Bois du St Quentin	July 27th	Contd.	In the afternoon Battn. moved up to BOIS DE COUTRON and bivouaced in the vicinity of the first H.Qrs. in the wood. No shelling in the immediate neighbourhood during the night, but scattered shelling was heard.	[illegible]
	28th		Morning overcast & foggy. Cleared later, but again became overcast. At 6 am. Battn. moved to take up assembly position on CHAUMUZY - NAPPES Rd. Position slightly altered en route. Battn. was not shelled on way up, but during the day there was constant shelling of ARDRE valley back to MARFAUX. Battn. position was not shelled till the afternoon. Battn. occupied position during the day, Bde. being in support, while the other two Brigades of Divn. followed enemy retirement with object of occupying entrenched line on West edge of BOIS DES ERCISSES. Lt. Dickson proceeded on leave. Strength going into line 15 Offrs. (including M.O.); 348 O.R. Battn. relieved the 153rd Infy. Bde. in the line. H.Qrs. in BOIS D'ECLISSES. Vicinity of H.Qrs. shelled.	[illegible]
	29th		Fine day. Battn. H.Qrs. shifted to hill overlooking CHAUMUZY. Gas bombardment about 10 p.m.	
	30th		Hazy morning but cleared to bright & warm day. After effects of gas bombardment caused much sickness amongst Coys. About 45 casualties. At 5.50 p.m. after 50 minutes preparatory bombardment French attacked on our left.	[illegible]
	31st		Very warm day. Enemy carried out harrassing shell fire all day long. The Battn. was relieved at night by 3rd Bn. French Infy. and proceeded to wood S of NATEUIL and bivouaced for night. Quiet relief and no casualties.	[illegible]

[illegible signature] Lieut. Colonel,
Commanding 9/4th Bn. Seaforth Hrs.

A5834 Wt. W4973/M687 750,000 8/16 D. D. & L. Ltd. Forms/C.2118/13.

(Confidential)

War Diary

of

1/4th. Battn. Seaforth Highrs.

(Volume 47)

from 1st August 1918.

to 31st. August 1918.

1/4th Bn. Seaforth Highrs.

Instructions regarding War Diaries and Intelligence Summaries are contained in F. S. Regs., Part II. and the Staff Manual respectively. Title pages will be prepared in manuscript.

WAR DIARY
or
~~INTELLIGENCE SUMMARY.~~
(Erase heading not required.)

Army Form C. 2118.

Place	Date	Hour	Summary of Events and Information	Remarks and references to Appendices
CHAMPILLON	1/8/18		Warm day. Battn moved to bivouacs in wood near CHAMPILLON. Remainder of the day spent in resting & cleaning up. Pay issued. Hostile aeroplanes were active during the night	JOR
	2/8/18		Dull day with a good deal of rain. Day spent in cleaning up & bathing in a pond in the wood	JOR
IN TRAIN	3/8/18		Battn moved off before dawn & entrained at EPERNAY Station. Train journey commenced at 6 a.m. In train all day	JOR
VILLERS BRULIN & BETHONSART	4/8/18		Battn detrained at BRIAS in the afternoon & proceeded in busses to VILLERS BRULIN & BETHONSART, Nos 1, 2 Coys & H.Q. in VILLERS BRULIN, Nos. 3 & 4 Coys. & Transport in BETHONSART.	JOR
	5/8/18		Dull day. Day spent in cleaning up & reorganising. Battn had baths at SAVY.	JOR
	6/8/18		Dull day. The C.O. inspected Coys. in the morning. Coys. carried out training in the afternoon	JOR
	7/8/18		Training carried on during the forenoon, demonstrations of ~~fight~~ fitting equipment. Gas drill, P.T., Musketry & Lewis Gun training.	JOR
	8/8/18		Dull day. Inspection of Box respirators. Training as on previous day.	JOR

D. D. & L., London, E.C.
(A8004) Wt. W1771/M2031 750,000 5/17 Sch. 52 Forms/C2118/14

Instructions regarding War Diaries and Intelligence Summaries are contained in F. S. Regs., Part II. and the Staff Manual respectively. Title pages will be prepared in manuscript.

WAR DIARY
or
~~INTELLIGENCE SUMMARY.~~
(Erase heading not required.)

Army Form C. 2118.

Place	Date	Hour	Summary of Events and Information	Remarks and references to Appendices
VILLERS BRULIN & BETHONSART	8/8/18		71 Other ranks, reinforcements and the following Officers joined the Battalion. 2 Lieuts, T.E. MACGREGOR, H.C. MILLER, A.B. BROWN, L.H.G. SYMINGTON, W.R. CULLEN, Captn & Quartermaster W.M. EADE, 2/6th Suffolk Regt. J.O.H.	
	9/8/18		Fine day. Inspection of Box respirators by Brigade Gas Officer. Training as on previous day. J.O.H.	
	10/8/18		Bright day. No 1 Coy on rifle range fired practices – Grouping, 100 yards. Application – Standing – 200 yds. Specialist classes in Scouting & Lewis Gun: Training otherwise as usual. 1 N.C.O. proceeded to G.H.Q. Lewis Gun Course. J.O.H.	
	11/8/18		Sunday. Fine day. Church parade at 11.30 a.m. in the open. C of E & R.C. Church parades separate: 2 Lt. W. Boardman D.C.M. rejoined from Hospital & 2 Lt. J.A. HOGG, reinforcement, joined the Battn. J.O.H.	
	12/8/18		Fine bright day. No 3 Coy on rifle range fired practices, Grouping, 100 yds. Application (Standing) 100 yds. Signalling class formed of all men who had had training in Signalling. Other specialist classes & training as before. J.O.H.	
	13/8/18		Fine bright day. No 2 Coy on Range fired practices as on 12th inst. Specialist classes & training as usual. Enemy aircraft very active over the area during the night & dropped several bombs. Lieut P.W. MACKENZIE joined the Battalion. J.O.H.	

D. D. & L., London, E.C. (A8004) Wt W1771/M2031 750,000 5/17 Sch. 52 Forms/C2118/14

Army Form C. 2118.

WAR DIARY
or
~~INTELLIGENCE SUMMARY.~~
(Erase heading not required.)

Instructions regarding War Diaries and Intelligence Summaries are contained in F. S. Regs., Part II. and the Staff Manual respectively. Title pages will be prepared in manuscript.

Place	Date	Hour	Summary of Events and Information	Remarks and references to Appendices
VILLERS BRULIN & BETHONSART	14/8/18		No. 4 Coy. on range fired the usual practises. Bad shots & casuals fired on the Range in the afternoon. Fine clear night & enemy aircraft again active, but no bombs dropped in the vicinity. J.O.R.	
FRONT LINE TRENCHES RIGHT SUB SECTOR GAVRELLE SECTOR	15/8/18		Fine bright day. Battn. entrained at SAVY about 3 pm. & proceeded by light railway to ECURIE Station. Transport moved by road. In the evening the Battn. relieved the 7th Scottish Rifles in right-sub sector of GAVRELLE Sector in the front line. Strength of Battn. going into the line – 22 Officers Medical Officer & 362 other ranks. No Echelon B. left out. Lewis Gun Officer, R.S.M. & a few details left at Transport lines. Front taken over was about 1000 yards. During the night 15th/16th enemy shelled behind Battn. lines with gas, a few shells dropping in Battn. area. J.O.R.	
	16/8/18		Fine bright day. Very little wind. Artillery activity intermittent on both sides. Our aircraft active, enemy less so. Patrol which went out at night to locate enemy was recalled on account of a gas projector discharge from lines of Battn. on our right. During night 16th/17th enemy shelled support line with gas, also areas behind. 2Lt. F. C. M. LANG & 2 N.C.Os. proceeded to 1st. Army Infantry School. 2 O.Rs. proceeded to 17th Corps Schools. 2Lt H. Paterson joined Battn. J.O.R.	

D. D. & L., London, E.C. (A8094) Wt W1771/M2031 750,000 5/17 Sch. 52 Forms/C2118/14

Instructions regarding War Diaries and Intelligence Summaries are contained in F. S. Regs., Part II. and the Staff Manual respectively. Title pages will be prepared in manuscript.

WAR DIARY
or
~~INTELLIGENCE SUMMARY.~~
(*Erase heading not required.*)

Army Form C. 2118.

Place	Date	Hour	Summary of Events and Information	Remarks and references to Appendices
FRONT LINE TRENCHES RIGHT SUB SECTOR GAVRELLE SECTOR	17/8/18		Dull day with fresh breeze changing from S.W. to W.N.W. Artillery fairly quiet on both sides. During night 17th/18th two Officers patrols went out to locate enemy positions. The first failed to get into touch with the enemy, the second consisting of an Officer and a platoon located enemy in their front line system through Machine gun fire and other signs. Officers & Other ranks proceeded to Divisional Classes lasting 14 days as follows. – 2Lt A.B.BROWN & 2 N.C.Os. Musketry – 2Lt T.E. MACGREGOR & 2 N.C.Os. Lewis Gun. – 2 N.C.Os. Bombing. 6 privates left for 4 weeks Divisional Class in Signalling. 2 N.C.Os proceeded to Divn. Classes as Instructors. JGH	
	18/8/18		Fine day, light westerly breeze. During the day our Artillery moderately active; enemy's very quiet, a little gas shelling at night. A small daylight patrol ~~discovered~~ located an enemy sentry in the front line & a Machine gun just behind. Two strong Officer's patrols went out during the night, the first gained no new information, the second reported that there were a number of posts in enemy's main front line trench. At the same time local operations took place on our right on both sides of the SCARPE in connection with ~~suspected~~ enemy retirement. The following joined Battn. in the line from Transport lines, 2Lt GREEN, Lewis Gun Officer, 2Lt H Paterson & R.S.M MASON. JGH	

D. D. & L., London, E.C. (A8004) Wt W1771/M2031 750,000 5/17 Sch. 52 Forms/C2118/14

Army Form C. 2118.

Instructions regarding War Diaries and Intelligence Summaries are contained in F. S. Regs., Part II. and the Staff Manual respectively. Title pages will be prepared in manuscript.

WAR DIARY
or
~~INTELLIGENCE SUMMARY.~~
(Erase heading not required.)

Place	Date	Hour	Summary of Events and Information	Remarks and references to Appendices
FRONT LINE TRENCHES	18/8/18		2Lt. J. S. FERGUSON proceeded to G.H.Q. Lewis Gun School. J.O.H.	
RIGHT-SUB SECTOR GAVRELLE SECTOR	19/8/18		Fine bright day, light westerly breeze changing to S.S.W. in the evening. Our artillery moderatively active, enemy's fairly quiet. One of our aeroplanes was seen to be brought down. At night a strong Officers patrol established the presence of enemy in THAMES ALLEY C.T. in front of his main front trench. During night 19th/20th gas discharges took place on our flanks. 2 Lieuts C. J. BOYD & F. J. CONWAY joined the Battn in the line. Enemy aircraft active during the night going to the rear areas. 2Lt. J. M. STURTON & 1 N.C.O. proceeded to 1st. Army Musketry Course. J.O.H.	
	20/8/18		Fine bright day, light South Westerly breeze falling away in the evening when it became misty. Our artillery moderatively active, enemy's quiet but active to our right during the night. Enemy aircraft active in the early morning. Small daylight patrol reconnoitred THAMES ALLEY C.T. across NO MANS LAND to ascertain what would be required to clear it of blocks etc. Battn. observers saw four enemy batteries in action. An enemy aeroplane fired on our front line with Machine Gun. Two night Officers patrols went out; the first, to confirm presence of enemy in THAMES ALLEY C.T., saw no J.O.H.	

D. D. & L., London, E.C. (A8004) Wt W1771/M2031 750,000 5/17 Sch. 52 Forms/C2118/14

Army Form C. 2118.

Instructions regarding War Diaries and Intelligence Summaries are contained in F. S. Regs., Part II. and the Staff Manual respectively. Title pages will be prepared in manuscript.

WAR DIARY
or
~~INTELLIGENCE SUMMARY.~~
(Erase heading not required.)

Place	Date	Hour	Summary of Events and Information	Remarks and references to Appendices
FRONT LINE TRENCHES RIGHT SUB SECTOR GAURELLE SECTOR	20/8/18		no signs of enemy there; visibility was bad owing to ground mist. The second patrol got in touch with enemy posts. During the night a gas discharge took place from front of Brigade on our left. Lieut. C.H. HODGSON, reinforcement & Captn. A. CAMPBELL from Rest Camp joined Battn. in the line. 2 Lt. D. KENNEDY rejoined from Hospital. J.O.H.	
	21/8/18		Very misty in the morning. Very warm day, light south easterly breeze. Our artillery active, enemy fairly quiet; ~~except for~~ a few gas shells fired in the morning. Our aircraft active, enemy's moderately so by day & very active during the night which was bright & moonlight, going towards the rear areas. Officers patrol at night heard enemy working in his front line trenches & was fired on by Machine guns. 2Lt. D. KENNEDY joined Battn. from Transport lines. 1 N.C.O. proceeded to 17th. Corps Gas School. 71 O.R. reinforcements joined the Battn. J.O.H.	
	22/8/18		Fine day, very hot with fresh southerly breeze. Our artillery active, enemy's quiet on our front but rather more active on our right ~~than~~ as is usually the case. Heavy firing heard to the South. Our aircraft very active, enemy's as usual much less so. Some movement of enemy aircraft to our rear areas at night. J.O.H.	

D. D. & L., London, E.C. (A8004) Wt W1771/M2051 750,000 5/17 Sch. 52 Forms/C2118/14

Army Form C. 2118.

Instructions regarding War Diaries and Intelligence Summaries are contained in F. S. Regs., Part II. and the Staff Manual respectively. Title pages will be prepared in manuscript.

WAR DIARY
or
~~INTELLIGENCE SUMMARY.~~

(Erase heading not required.)

Place	Date	Hour	Summary of Events and Information	Remarks and references to Appendices
FRONT LINE TRENCHES	22/8/18		Strong Officers patrol went out at night, but its operations were hampered by Artillery fire on to No MANS LAND. Lieut. A.A. FINNIGAN went to Hospital Sick. J.O.H.	
RIGHT SUB SECTOR. GAVRELLE SECTOR.	23/8/18		Fine day, not so hot, very slight northerly wind. Our artillery active, but rather less than previous day, enemy's quiet on our front. Some gas shelling on our left. Brigade on our right carried out a local attack in the early morning. Aircraft activity as usual. No patrolling was done. 1 N.C.O. proceeded to 1st. Army Signalling School. J.O.H.	
	24/8/18		Fine day, very light northerly breeze, becoming quite calm at night. Our artillery fairly active, principally on areas to right of our front. Enemy's more active than usual on our front & fairly active to our right. During the night considerable gas shelling on our immediate right. Our aircraft active, enemy more active than usual by day & continuing the activity usual at night, moonlight being still bright. A small daylight patrol up THAMES ALLEY C.T. found signs of recent occupation. Two Officers patrols were out at night; one, for general purposes, did not come into contact with enemy, the other reconnoitred & cleared C.T. across No. MANS LAND in preparation for an operation the following morning. An aeroplane, nationality unknown, was seen to come down in flames in our lines to our right. J.O.H.	

D. D. & L., London, E.C. (A8094) Wt W1771/M2031 750,000 5/17 Sch. 52 Forms/C2118/14

Army Form C. 2118.

Instructions regarding War Diaries and Intelligence Summaries are contained in F. S. Regs., Part II. and the Staff Manual respectively. Title pages will be prepared in manuscript.

WAR DIARY

or

~~INTELLIGENCE SUMMARY.~~

(Erase heading not required.)

Place	Date	Hour	Summary of Events and Information	Remarks and references to Appendices
FRONT LINE TRENCHES RIGHT SUB SECTOR GAVRELLE SECTOR.	25/8/18		Fine day. In conjunction with an advance by the two right Brigades of the Division, one Coy. No 3 Coy. moved up from Support & took over a part of front line from Battn. on our right, then advanced about 1000 yds. along with attacking Units & formed a defensive flank on left of their position. During the day the position was subjected to constant sniping. A counter attack by the enemy compelled withdrawal. The position was regained early the following morning. Our artillery very active, enemy's active especially on new positions. Our aircraft active, enemy's not more than usual & less active at night, it being overcast. Daylight patrol went up C.T. to left of new positions to harass enemy firing on it. JOH	
	26/8/18		Fine day. Advanced position lost the previous day was recovered early in the morning by No. 3 Coy. Later the operations were continued, 6th. Black Watch attacking on our right & our No 2 Coy advancing on their left past No 3 Coy. & forming a defensive flank on the left of the new position obtained, depth of advance about 500 yards. This operation was completed by 1.30 pm. At 7pm. in conjunction with a further advance of troops on our right our No 4 Coy. advanced & continued the defensive flank beyond No. 2 Coy., being in position about 9-40 pm. During the afternoon No 3 Coy. was reorganized in depth behind JOH	

D. D. & L., London, E.C. (A8004) W1 W1771/M2031 750,000 5/17 Sch. 52 Forms/C2118/14

Army Form C. 2118.

WAR DIARY
or
~~INTELLIGENCE SUMMARY.~~
(Erase heading not required.)

Instructions regarding War Diaries and Intelligence Summaries are contained in F. S. Regs., Part II. and the Staff Manual respectively. Title pages will be prepared in manuscript.

Place	Date	Hour	Summary of Events and Information	Remarks and references to Appendices
FRONT LINE TRENCHES RIGHT SUB SECTOR GAVRELLE SECTOR	26/8/18		Nos. 4 & 2 Coys. on right of the GAVRELLE Road. Meantime No. 1 Coy. was organized in depth on left of the road, mainly in advance of our old front line, being in touch on its left with 7th. A & S. Hrs. who had side stepped to the right as 4th Seaforths moved forward. During the night Nos. 2 & 4 Coys. pushed forward strong patrols & established advanced posts in trenches to the right of GAVRELLE without opposition. Our artillery active, enemy's active in the morning & again in the evening. Our aircraft active, enemy's only very moderately so.	J.D.H.
	27/8/18		Dull day, some rain. During the day No 2 Coy. withdrew from the advanced posts occupied the previous day, owing to the 7th. A & S. Hrs. being forced to withdraw from advanced posts which they had occupied on our left. Later these posts were re-occupied. Otherwise the day was normal. During the night the Battalion was relieved by 2nd. Bn. East Lancs. Rgt. & moved back to dugouts in ARRAS - BAILLEUL Railway cutting just N. of River SCARPE.	J.D.H.
DUG-OUTS IN RESERVE ARRAS - BAILLEUL Railway Cutting	28/8/18		Dull day, occasional showers. At night Battn. moved up into 153rd Infy. Brigade Sector of the line, S. of ARRAS - GAVRELLE Road in support of 4th Gordon Hrs. & 7th. A & S. Hrs. in the front line. Two Coys. remained at Battn. H.Q., the other two went further forward. Lieut. H.C. BESSANT, reinforcement joined the Battn.	J.D.H.

D. D. & L., London, E.C.
(A8001) Wt. W1771/M2031 750,000 5/17 Sch. 52 Forms/C2118/14

Instructions regarding War Diaries and Intelligence Summaries are contained in F. S. Regs., Part II. and the Staff Manual respectively. Title pages will be prepared in manuscript.

WAR DIARY

or

~~INTELLIGENCE SUMMARY.~~

(Erase heading not required.)

Army Form C. 2118.

Place	Date	Hour	Summary of Events and Information	Remarks and references to Appendices
SUPPORT LINE NR. ROEUX	29/8/18		Fine day, following night exceptionally dark. At 6.30 a.m. front Battns. attacked GREENLAND HILL with 4th Seaforth Hrs. in Brigade Reserve. The Battn. did not come into action, the attack being successful. Our artillery covered the attack with a barrage & was active throughout the day & night. Enemy retaliation to the barrage was not strong but artillery was fairly active during the day & night. Our aircraft fairly active, the enemy more active than usual. At night the two Coys. at Battn. H.Q. moved forward to a position in front of the other two to conform to the advance of the front line. Working parties were ordered by Brigade from the latter two Coys. & proceeded, but no work was done owing to the lateness of receipt of orders & darkness of the night.	J.H.
	30/8/18		Fine day, westerly wind, some rain the following night. Front Battns. pushed front line forward, 4th Seaforths did not move. Our artillery fairly active, but not so active as previous day. Enemy artillery also less active. Our aircraft active both day & night. Enemy aircraft modrately active. At night bombs were dropped in the vicinity.	J.H.

D. D. & L., London, E.C. (A8004) Wt W1771/M2031 750,000 5/17 Sch. 52 Forms/C2118/14

Army Form C. 2118.

Instructions regarding War Diaries and Intelligence Summaries are contained in F. S. Regs., Part II. and the Staff Manual respectively. Title pages will be prepared in manuscript.

WAR DIARY
or
~~INTELLIGENCE~~ SUMMARY.

(Erase heading not required.)

Place	Date	Hour	Summary of Events and Information	Remarks and references to Appendices
SUPPORT LINE NR. ROEUX	31/8/18		Fine day; westerly breeze. Front line remained as before. Our artillery moderatively active. Enemy's active in the afternoon & by night, partly in search for our advanced batteries, which the capture of high ground had allowed to move forward. Our aircraft active as usual; Enemy's active in the late afternoon flying low over our lines, engaged by Stokes Mortars & Lewis Guns. Patrols of left front Battn. up C.Ts. at night reported opposition. Information received so far appears to show that enemy is holding FRESNES–BOUVROY line – 800 to 1500 yards in front of our present line – in strength, with a line of outposts in front.	
			J.O. Hopkinson Lt. Col. Comdg. 4th Seaforth Highrs.	

D. D. & L., London, E.C.
(A8004) Wt W1771/M2031 750,000 5/17 Sch. 52 Forms/C2118/14

154/51

(Confidential)

War Diary

of

1/4th. Battn. Seaforth Highlanders.

(Volume 48)

from 1st September 1918

to 30th. September 1918.

1/4th Bn. Seaforth Highrs.

Instructions regarding War Diaries and Intelligence Summaries are contained in F. S. Regs., Part II. and the Staff Manual respectively. Title pages will be prepared in manuscript.

WAR DIARY
or
~~INTELLIGENCE SUMMARY.~~
(Erase heading not required.)

154/51 WO 95/36 [handwritten reference]

Army Form C. 2118.

Place	Date	Hour	Summary of Events and Information	Remarks and references to Appendices
LEFT SUB SECTOR GREENLAND HILL SECTOR FRONT LINE	1/9/18		Fine day. South westerly breeze. Enemy artillery fairly quiet on Battalion area - occasional shelling; our artillery active. Our aircraft active; enemy aircraft unusually active; over 40 planes being over our lines during the day. A long range gun & a light battery were located by Battn. observers. During night 1/2nd the Battn relieved 1/7th Argyle & Sutherland Highrs. in left sub sector of the Brigade front three companies in front, one (No 3 Coy) in support.	
	2/9/18		Fine day. Our artillery very active, 60 pounder guns were firing from vicinity of and in front of Battn. H.Q., drawing some reply from the enemy. Battn. front was subjected to considerable shelling, including gas. Our aircraft very active. Enemy's also active, crossing our lines repeatedly particularly during the afternoon, on one occasion flying very low. Three of our observation baloons were seen to be brought down in flames. Three patrols went out along communication trenches in the evening to ascertain enemy dispositions with the view of our forces occupying the FRESNES - ROUVROY line if not held in force. The enemy appeared to be holding it firmly with outposts in front & no offensive action was undertaken.	
	3/9/18		Fine day. Our artillery active. Our positions were again subjected to considerable shelling. Aircraft on both sides active. Early in the morning a low flying plane observed battery positions of ours and was over our lines for some time without	

D. D. & L., London, E.C. (A8604) Wt W1771/M2031 750,000 5/17 Sch. 52 Forms/C2118/14

4HS 7 sheets

Instructions regarding War Diaries and Intelligence Summaries are contained in F. S. Regs., Part II. and the Staff Manual respectively. Title pages will be prepared in manuscript.

WAR DIARY
or
~~INTELLIGENCE SUMMARY.~~
(Erase heading not required.)

Army Form C. 2118.

Place	Date	Hour	Summary of Events and Information	Remarks and references to Appendices
LEFT SUB SECTOR. GREENLAND HILL SECTOR FRONT LINE	3/9/18		molestation. During night 2nd/3rd Battn. was relieved by 1/5th Yorks & Lancs. and moved back to WAKEFIELD CAMP near ROCLINCOURT, 154 th Infantry Brigade going into Divisional Reserve. J.R.	
WAKEFIELD Camp ROCLINCOURT	4/9/18		Fine day. Day spent in resting & cleaning up. 210 O.R reinforcements joined the Battn. J.R.	
	5/9/18		Fine day. Coys. parade for kit inspection & cleaning up. The new draft was inspected by C.O., had standing orders read out to it & was tested in drill under R.S.M. A nightly aeroplane piquet was ordered. J.R.	
	6/9/18		Fine day. Very warm with threatening of thunderstorm. N.C.Os parade before breakfast under R.S.M. Battn. parade at 8.45 am Training as follows was carried out by Coys.:- P.T. & B.T., Gas drill, Close order drill musketry. Coy. schemes in Open warfare. Specialist classes for Scouts & Snipers, Lewis Gunners, Signallers & Stretcher bearers was carried on, specialists joining their Coys. for open warfare training. C.O. inspected No. 1 Coy. Officers classes in map reading Lewis Gun & Riding in the afternoon. J.R.	
	7/9/18		Fine in the morning thunderstorm with heavy rain later. Parades & training as before but no Officers classes. C.O. inspected No 2 Coy. Bde. Gas. N.C.O. inspected Box respirators. J.R.	

D. D. & L., London, E.C. (A8004) Wt W1771/M2031 750,000 5/17 Sch. 52 Forms/C2118/14

Army Form C. 2118.

Instructions regarding War Diaries and Intelligence Summaries are contained in F. S. Regs., Part II. and the Staff Manual respectively. Title pages will be prepared in manuscript.

WAR DIARY
or
~~INTELLIGENCE SUMMARY.~~
(Erase heading not required.)

Place	Date	Hour	Summary of Events and Information	Remarks and references to Appendices
WAKEFIELD Camp	8/9/18		Sunday. Wet day on the whole. Church parades for Presbyterians, C of Es & R.Cs. Inspection of Box respirators by Bde. Gas N.C.O. complete. J.S.H.	
ROCLINCOURT	9/9/18		Unsettled day with some rain. Parades & training as usual. No 1 Coy. carried out attack practise finishing with a field practise on range in the afternoon. J.S.H.	
	10/9/18		Unsettled day. High wind & intermittent heavy rain. Parades & training interrupted by rain in the forenoon. No 2 Coy carried out practise as No. 1 Coy. on the previous day. J.S.H.	
LANCASTER CAMP	11/9/18		Unsettled day, some rain. In the afternoon Battn. moved to LANCASTER Camp near MOUNT ST. ELOY, 51st (Highland) Division being relieved by 49th Division in the line. J.S.H.	
MT ST ELOY.	12/9/18		Very wet. All training except such as could be carried on indoors stopped by the rain. J.S.H.	
	13/9/18		Weather improved. Training in Musketry, drill & Gas & P.T. & B.T. carried on in the forenoon also specialist classes as before. Coys. carried out schemes for open warfare. Nos. 1 & 2 Coys. practicing advancing under a barrage. J.S.H.	
	14/9/18		Fine day. Nos 1, 2 & 4 Coys. carried out schemes in open warfare on training area. No 3 Coy. fired on BRAY RANGE - grouping - application (at 200 yds.) & rapid (at 200 yds) practises fired. J.S.H.	

D. D & L., London, E.C.
(A8004) Wt W1771/M2031 750,000 5/17 Sch. 52 Forms/C2118/14

Army Form C. 2118.

WAR DIARY
or
~~INTELLIGENCE SUMMARY.~~
(Erase heading not required.)

Instructions regarding War Diaries and Intelligence Summaries are contained in F. S. Regs., Part II, and the Staff Manual respectively. Title pages will be prepared in manuscript.

Place	Date	Hour	Summary of Events and Information	Remarks and references to Appendices
LANCASTER CAMP MT. ST. ELOY	15/9/18		Sunday. Fine warm day. Brigade church parade at 10.30 a.m. Battn. had baths at MT. ST. ELOY. G.O.C. Division inspected Battn. Transport at 2 p.m.	J.S.H.
	16/9/18		Warm day. Muster parade of Battn. at 8.30 a.m., thereafter No. 4 Coy. fired on BRAY RANGE, practices as on 14th inst. G.O.C. Division viewed the Coys. at training.	J.S.H.
	17/9/18		Fine day. G.O.C. Division inspected No. 2 Coy. on parade ground. The other Coys. carried out training in musketry, rifle bombing & open warfare schemes on training area.	J.S.H.
	18/9/18		Cold morning. Coys. carry out usual training on training area. Specialist classes as usual.	J.S.H.
	19/9/18		Fine day but cold. North Easterly gale. Coys. carried out training as Outpost Coys. on training area. Specialist classes as usual.	J.S.H.
	20/9/18		Heavy rain during morning. Fine during afternoon and rain again in late evening. Coys. carried out usual training on MOUNT ST. ELOY Area and No 3 Coy. gave demonstration of "Cooperation of Infantry with Tanks." Specialist classes as usual.	J.S.H.
	21/9/18		Showery during morning and afternoon. Usual Coy. training. Classes as usual.	J.S.H.
	22/9/18		Weather cold & showery. Battn. prepared for moving into the line at 1 p.m. These orders were cancelled at about 11 a.m.	J.S.H.

D. D & L., London, E.C. (A8004) Wt W1771/M2031 750,000 5/17 Sch. 52 Forms/C2118/14

Instructions regarding War Diaries and Intelligence Summaries are contained in F. S. Regs., Part II. and the Staff Manual respectively. Title pages will be prepared in manuscript.

WAR DIARY
or
~~INTELLIGENCE SUMMARY.~~
(Erase heading not required.)

Army Form C. 2118.

Place	Date	Hour	Summary of Events and Information	Remarks and references to Appendices
LANCASTER CAMP	23/9/18		Cold & showery. Usual training on area & parade ground. Specialist classes as usual. J.H.	
	24/9/18		Frosty morning & misty. Battn. prepared for moving into the line at 1 p.m.	
MT ST ELOY.			Battn. relieved the 5th Bn. Yorks & Lancs, 49th Division in the left sub sector GREENLAND HILL Sector. Quiet relief, no casualties. J.H.	
	25/9/18		Fine day. Enemy shelling whole area. A few casualties in Support Coy. Our artillery active carrying out various shoots. J.H.	
	26/9/18		Cold & frosty morning. Warm during day. Enemy artillery carried out harassing fire over Battn. area. During early morning our batteries were shelled with gas shells. Coys. engaged patrolling & repairing trenches during dark. J.H.	
	27/9/18		Rain & dull during morning. Fine later on. The Division carried out a "Chinese attack" in conjunction with attack on left. No enemy retaliation & attack on left appeared to progress favourably. No targets were damaged in "Chinese attack." Patrols sent out and ascertained enemy held FRESNES Line & also held positions forward in vicinity of WICK Trench. Working party located in HOLLOW. COPSE. Coys. busy repairing trenches. During Chinese attack light was very bad and it is extremely doubtful if enemy could see dummies. J.H.	

D. D & L., London, E.C.
(A8004) Wt W1771/M2031 750,000 5/17 Sch. 52 Forms/C2118/14

Instructions regarding War Diaries and Intelligence Summaries are contained in F. S. Regs., Part II. and the Staff Manual respectively. Title pages will be prepared in manuscript.

WAR DIARY
or
~~INTELLIGENCE SUMMARY.~~
(Erase heading not required.)

Army Form C. 2118.

Place	Date	Hour	Summary of Events and Information	Remarks and references to Appendices
LEFT SUB SECTOR GREENLAND HILL SECTOR.	28/9/18		Dull morning. In forenoon heavy rain. Patrols sent out in early morning were fired on from HOLLOW COPSE & WICK TRENCH. Two men missing. Captn. W.S. Dane M.C. Adjutant proceeded on leave.	
FRONT LINE	29/9/18		Fine morning. Patrols sent out in early morning located two BOCHE posts. but could not get near enough to wire to report on state of same owing to enemy snipers. Coy. constructing & repairing fire positions during night. Heavy rain set in at 6.30 pm. Heavy artillery cutting wire in front of FRESNES line all day.	
	30/9/18		Cold morning & heavy rain. Battn. H.Q. heavily shelled. Patrols active but little to report. ~~Gas projector attack on our front by R.Es. 300 projectors fired [illegible].~~	

J.O. Hopkinson Lieut. Col.
Commanding
4th. Bn. Seaforth Highrs.

D. D & L., London, E.C. (A8004) Wt W1771/M2031 750,000 5/17 Sch. 52 Forms/C2118/14

45S
15 sheets

Confidential

Vol 37

War Diary

of

1/4th Battn. Seaforth Highlanders

(Volume 49)

From - 1st October 1918
To - 31st October 1918.

Instructions regarding War Diaries and Intelligence Summaries are contained in F. S. Regs., Part II. and the Staff Manual respectively. Title pages will be prepared in manuscript.

WAR DIARY
or
~~INTELLIGENCE SUMMARY.~~
(Erase heading not required.)

Army Form C. 2118.

Place	Date	Hour	Summary of Events and Information	Remarks and references to Appendices
In the Line GREENLAND HILL.	1/10/18		Cold day. Night and day patrols were sent out by us and ascertained the enemy still held FRESNES LINE. On night of 1st/2nd Battn. was relieved by 2nd Bn. Rifle Bde, 8th Div. and embussed at ATHIES for LANCASTER CAMP, MONT. ST ELOY. Last of Battn. arrived in camp at 07-30hrs. [initials]	
MONT ST. ELOY.	2/10/18		Cold morning but cleared up to fine day. Battalion resting in the morning. Cleaning up in the afternoon. Draft of 81 O.Ranks joined the Battn. [initials]	
	3/10/18		Fine day. Coys. cleaning up and kit inspections held. Battalion had baths at ECOIVRES. [initials]	
	4/10/18		Dull and windy day. Companies carrying out training on training areas. S.B.R. Inspection by Brigade Gas N.C.O. [initials]	

(A9173) Wt W2358/P360 600,000 12/17 D. D. & L. Sch. 52a. Forms/C2118/15.

Instructions regarding War Diaries and Intelligence Summaries are contained in F. S. Regs., Part II, and the Staff Manual respectively. Title pages will be prepared in manuscript.

WAR DIARY
or
~~INTELLIGENCE SUMMARY.~~
(Erase heading not required.)

Army Form C. 2118.

Place	Date	Hour	Summary of Events and Information	Remarks and references to Appendices
MONT. ST ELOY.	5/10/18.		Dull and windy day. Usual training carried out. Inspection of rifles by Brigade Armourer Sergt. Warning Order for Division to move to CAMBRAI Sector on 7/8th inst. received.	
	6/10/18.		Cold morning. Dull & windy day. Divine service for all denominations.	
	7/10/18		Dull and wet day. Battn. embussed at MONT ST ELOY at 18.00 hrs but did not commence journey till 21.00 hrs.	
INCHY	8/10/18.		Cold morning. The Battalion debussed at INCHY about 04.00 hrs. Resting and cleaning up.	
	9/10/18.		Cold and misty morning but cleared up to fine day. Companies carry out training near Headqrs. Inspection of Iron Rations, Field Dressings and Identity discs. 2/Lt. Clark & Bn. Scouts reconnoitre roads to BOURLON for transport.	

(A9173) Wt W2358/P360 600,000 12/17 D. D. & L. Sch. 52a. Forms/C2118/15.

Instructions regarding War Diaries and Intelligence Summaries are contained in F. S. Regs., Part II. and the Staff Manual respectively. Title pages will be prepared in manuscript.

WAR DIARY
or
~~INTELLIGENCE~~ SUMMARY.
(*Erase heading not required.*)

Army Form C. 2118.

Place	Date	Hour	Summary of Events and Information	Remarks and references to Appendices
INCHY.	10/10/18		Dull morning but cleared up to fine day. Battn. moved from INCHY to NEUVILLE St REMY on outskirts of CAMBRAI and relieved the 4th C.M.R., of 3rd Canadian Division. Balloon taken down by enemy aeroplane. H.V. shelling in vicinity of Battn. H.Qrs, one shell landing at corner of house killing 6 and wounding 13 of R.F.A. & R.E. and killing 6 horses.	
	11/10/18.		Cold and dull morning, later drizzle. Orders received to prepare to move, probable destination being the line. Later orders Division to relieve 2nd Canadian Division. The Battn. moved to the line in front of IWUY at 22.00hrs. Battn. H.Qrs. in village. Relieved the 24th Bn. Canadian Infantry. Shelled on way up but no casualties. Several casualties in ration party.	
IWUY.	12/10/18.		Cold morning. Village heavily shelled. Two Huns found in cellars in the village. The Corps in conjunction with Corps on right and left attacked at 12.00 hr. 157 Bde on right and 154 Bde on left representing our Division. Battn. disposed as follows. Nos. 1, 2 & 3 Coys in front. No. 4 Coy.	

(A9175) Wt W2358/P360 600,000 12/17 D. D. & L. Sch. 52a. Forms/C2118/15.

Army Form C. 2118.

Instructions regarding War Diaries and Intelligence Summaries are contained in F. S. Regs., Part II. and the Staff Manual respectively. Title pages will be prepared in manuscript.

WAR DIARY
or
INTELLIGENCE SUMMARY.
(*Erase heading not required.*)

Place	Date	Hour	Summary of Events and Information	Remarks and references to Appendices
IWUY	12/10/18	Contd.	in support. Advance proceeded without much opposition until Coys reached ridge 100 yards in front of objective. Here machine gun fire was encountered but Coys passed quickly over ridge and consolidated on objectives. 7th A. & S. Hrs. passed through our Battn with objective of LIEU ST AMAND. Machine gun fire delayed their advance on the left and they were unable to capture the village. Battn. H.Qrs. moved to O.24.a.1.1.	
			Casualties - Officers - 1 Killed & 1 Wounded. O.R. - 5 Killed and 61 wounded.	
			Coys. readjusted and disposed with Nos. 3 & 4 in front and Nos. 1 & 2 in support.	
	13/10/18		Cold and dull day: raining in the morning. In conjunction with 49th Division we attacked today. Divisional objective - FLEURY and NOYELLES-SUR-SELLE. 7th A. & S. Hrs. advanced behind barrage at 09.00 hrs but met with severe M.G. and artillery fire and were unable to reach their objective. No. 3 Coy. pushed forward their line on right in face of very heavy M.G. fire and captured LA MOTTE BLANCHE FARM. Enemy artillery very active all day shelling all Battn. area with H.Es and Gas. During today's	

(A9175) Wt W2358/P360 600,000 12/17 D. D. & L. **Sch. 52a.** Forms/C2118/15.

Instructions regarding War Diaries and Intelligence Summaries are contained in F. S. Regs., Part II. and the Staff Manual respectively. Title pages will be prepared in manuscript.

WAR DIARY
or
~~INTELLIGENCE SUMMARY.~~
(*Erase heading not required.*)

Army Form C. 2118.

Place	Date	Hour	Summary of Events and Information	Remarks and references to Appendices
	13/10/18	Contd.	Todays operations we captured 3 enemy M.G.s, using one against the enemy. [initials]	
	14/10/18.		Cold and misty. Enemy artillery very active shelling with all calibres and Gas. Three direct hits on Battn. H.Qrs. 2/Lt. F. C. Clark & artillery liaison officer killed, Lt. Col. Hopkinson wounded and Capt. & A/Adjt. D. Campbell gassed. Several O.R. casualties. Capt. Geo. H. Macpherson took over command and Lieut. A. E. F. Macgregor acted as adjutant. Bn. was relieved by 6th A. & S. H[rs]. 153 Brigade. Quiet relief and no casualties. Battn. proceeded to billets in THUN ST MARTIN. [initials]	
THUN ST. MARTIN	15/10/18		Brigade in Divisional Reserve. Cold day and dull. Enemy shelling vicinity with H.Vs. and gas shells. Major L. D. Henderson, M.C. rejoined from Div. Reception Camp and took over command of the Battn. Inspection of Iron Rations, Field Dressings and Identity Discs. [initials]	
	16/10/18.		Raining and cold. Coys. at disposal of Coy. Commanders. Warning order to relieve)	

Instructions regarding War Diaries and Intelligence Summaries are contained in F. S. Regs., Part II. and the Staff Manual respectively. Title pages will be prepared in manuscript.

WAR DIARY or INTELLIGENCE SUMMARY.

(Erase heading not required.)

Army Form C. 2118.

Place	Date	Hour	Summary of Events and Information	Remarks and references to Appendices
THUN ST MARTIN	16/10/18	contd	relieve 152 Bde. in the line received.	FH
	17/10/18		Dull and cold morning. Reorganising of Coys. ½ hours Gas drill and 1 hours Salvage. The Battn. relieved the 6/7th Gordon Hrs. in Bde. reserve at SE. corner of IWUY. No casualties. Area heavily shelled with gas during the night.	FH
IWUY	18/10/18		Very misty: hard frost. Enemy artillery active during the morning.	
	19/10/18		Misty in early morning. Enemy artillery active. Gas sent over with H.V. shells.	FH
	20/10/18		Weather good but cold. No. 384 Coy. went forward to AVESNES-LE-SEC at 13.30hrs. No. 172 Coy. to left of village. No. 374 Coys 500 yards behind village. As the enemy withdrew 3 hours later, orders were received from Bde at 15.30hrs and Battalion went forward immediately. Concentrated at Cross Roads with Railway - O.10.c.3.1. at 02.20hrs. Coys. were given orders at 02.30hrs. to move	
	21/10/18		to assembly positions across the River SELLE. Coys. formed up 100 yards in front of/	

(A9175) Wt W2358/P360 600,000 12/17 D. D. & L. Sch. 52a. Forms/C2118/15.

Instructions regarding War Diaries and Intelligence Summaries are contained in F. S. Regs., Part II. and the Staff Manual respectively. Title pages will be prepared in manuscript.

WAR DIARY
or
INTELLIGENCE SUMMARY.
(Erase heading not required.)

Army Form C. 2118.

Place	Date	Hour	Summary of Events and Information	Remarks and references to Appendices
	21/10/18	Contd.	of River. Coys in assembly positions by 04·45 hrs. Coys moved forward from their positions at 05·20 hrs encountering heavy M.G. fire from 2 Machine Guns in position 300 yards to the left of MON ROUGE Farm. By flanking movements by platoons this was overcome and enemy gun teams scattered. Joint H.Qrs with Argylls established in Chateau in NOYELLES. Heavy rain the whole night.	[illegible]
	22/10/18		Fine day. The Battalion was relieved by 4th Black Watch and moved to billets in DOUCHY.	[illegible]
DOUCHY.	23/10/18		Enemy shelling outskirts during early morning. Fine day. Forenoon devoted to resting and cleaning up. Batt. moved in the afternoon to outskirts of DENAIN. Coys billeted in mill on the bank of CANAL DE L'ESCAUT.	[illegible]
DENAIN.	24/10/18		Bright day. DENAIN shelled with H.Vs. Day devoted to cleaning up. Kit inspections under Coy arrangements.	[illegible]
	25/10/18		Fine day. Companies on Gas, Physical and Musketry training.	[illegible]

(A9175) Wt W2358/P360 600,000 12/17 D. D. & L. Sch. 52a. Forms/C2118/15.

Instructions regarding War Diaries and Intelligence Summaries are contained in F. S. Regs., Part II. and the Staff Manual respectively. Title pages will be prepared in manuscript.

WAR DIARY
or
~~INTELLIGENCE SUMMARY.~~
(Erase heading not required.)

Army Form C. 2118.

Place	Date	Hour	Summary of Events and Information	Remarks and references to Appendices
DENAIN	26/10/18		Fine day. S.B.R. inspection by Brigade Gas N.C.O. Battalion moved up the line to a position in I.14.d. and remained in this position until 04.00hrs the following morning.	
	27/10/18		Fine day but rain set in at night. Battn. moved at 04.00 hrs into the line relieving the 6th Argylls. During relief enemy shelling left Coy very heavily. Also machine gun fire from factories across CANAL. Coys. disposed Nos 1, 2 & 4 in front; No. 3 in support. Battn. H.Qrs. at CHATEAU DE PRES.	
	28/10/18		Fine day but wet. The Division attacked at 05.15 hrs. Objective of the Battn. was on other side of road leading from POIRIER STN to AULNOY. The attack was ~~[illegible]~~ successful but the enemy counter attacked immediately and forced us back to southern outskirts of wood MONT HOUY. We took 180 prisoners and 21 machine guns. Enemy lost heavily in killed and wounded. Battn. started off with Nos 1, 2 & 4 in front and No. 3 in support. On completion of operation all Coys were in front. 6th Argylls relieved the Battn. and Coys moved back to positions near Battn. H.Qrs. Casualties – Officers – 2 killed, 5 wounded and 2 missing.	

(A9175) Wt W2358/P360 600,000 12/17 D. D. & L. Sch. 52a. Forms/C2118/15.

Army Form C. 2118.

Instructions regarding War Diaries and Intelligence Summaries are contained in F. S. Regs., Part II. and the Staff Manual respectively. Title pages will be prepared in manuscript.

WAR DIARY
or
INTELLIGENCE SUMMARY.
(Erase heading not required.)

Place	Date	Hour	Summary of Events and Information	Remarks and references to Appendices
	28/10/18 contd		O Ranks - Killed 4, wounded 12, missing 44.	
	29/10/18.		Dull day. Battn moved back to billets in MILL on outskirts of DENAIN. Coys. all in by 11.00 hrs	
	30/10/18		Dull day. Coys. cleaning and kit inspections. During morning enemy shelled DENAIN with H.Vs.	
	31/10/18		Dull & cold day. Raining in afternoon. Battn moved back to billets in ESCAUDOEVRES and arrived at 15.30 hrs.	

[illegible] Major,
Commanding, 4th Bn. Seaforth Highlanders.

1/4th.Bn.Seaforth Highlanders.

HISTORY OF OPERATIONS

from night of 11th. to night of 14/15th.October 1918.

On the night of the 11th./12th. October 1918 the Battalion took over from 27th.Canadian Infantry Battalion - 3 Coys. in front line and one in support.

The front line extended from 0.25.c.[illegible].0 to N.30.a.1.3. and the support Company occupied a line running from N.36.b.3.0 to N.36.a.80.25.

At 12.10 hours on the 12th.October the Battalion received orders to advance and consolidate on a line running from 0.14.a.2.1. to N.18.a.2.[illegible]. The Battalion met with little opposition until it reached ridge 100 yards behind objective. Here it came under heavy machine gun fire from village of LIEU St. AMAND but Coys. moved quickly over the ridge and consolidated on forward slope as above stated.

The support Coy. (No.4 Coy.) consolidated 150 yards behind ridge from 0.13.a.8.1. to N.18.b.5.3. - two platoons on right and two on left.

About 02.00 hours on the 13th.October orders were received that the Battalion frontage would be from 0.14.a.3.6. to 0.13.a.70.95. To conform with this ~~No.4 Coy. took over the front line~~ No. 3 Coy. and No. 4 Coy. took over the front line and Nos. 1 & 2 Coys. moved into support behind the road from 0.13.d.[illegible].8. to 0.13.a.4.3.

This was to be the jumping off position for Battalion in the attack on NOYELLES SUR SELLE at 0[illegible].45 hours on 13th .Octr. in the event of the attack by 7th.Bn.A.& S.Hrs. on LIEU. St. AMAND being a success.

At 0[illegible].00 hours the 7th.A.& S.Hrs. moved forward to attack the village of LIEU ST.AMAND but were held up by heavy machine gun fire from the village.

In consequence of this No.4 Coy. on our left front did not advance. No. 3 Coy., however found it possible to advance on Mon. BLANCHE FARM and consolidate on either side of it being in touch with 152nd.Infy.Brigade on their right.

In the taking of this farm No. 3 Coy. met with intense enfilade Machine gun fire from the village of LIEU ST.AMAND and the wood 500 yards on their right. Before reaching the FARM a great proportion of the N.C.Os. of the Coy. became casualties . The Company Commander and the Coy.Sergt. Major however collected the remainder of the Company and advanced again on the farm and occupied it.

The line now taken up by the Battalion ran from 0.8.a.88.20 to 0.13.a.70.95. ,support Coys. remaining in original positions

The Battalion was relieved on the night of the 14th./15th. October 1918 by the 6th.Bn.A.& S.Highrs.

During these operations the following casualties occurred.

<u>OFFICERS.</u>

Killed	2.	Wounded	2.	Wounded (Gas)	1.

<u>OTHER RANKS.</u>

Killed	21.	Wounded	[illegible]1.	Wounded (Gas)	6
				Missing	2.

Major,
Comdg.4th.Bn.Seaforth Highrs.

2888

154 BDE

HISTORY OF OPERATIONS

by

1/4th Battalion THE SEAFORTH HIGHLANDERS.

11th - 15th October.

On the night of the 11/12th October, 1918, the Battalion took over from 27th Canadian Infantry Battalion - 3 companies in front line and one in support.

The front line extended from O.25.c.9.0. to N.30.a.1.3. and the support company occupied a line running from N.36.b.3.0. to N.36.a.80.25.

At 12.10 hours on the 12th October, the Battalion received orders to advance and consolidate on a line running from O.14.a.2.1. to N.18.A.2.9. The battalion met with little opposition until it reached ridge 100 yards behind objective. Here it came under heavy machine gun fire from village of LIEU ST.AMAND but companies moved quickly over the ridge and consolidated on forward slope as above stated.

The support company (No.4) consolidated 150 yards behind ridge from O.13.a.8.1. to N.18.b.5.3. - two platoons on right of road and two on left.

About 02.00 hours on the 13th October orders were received that the battalion frontage would be from O.14.a.3.6. to O.13.a.70.95. To conform with this No.3 Company and No.4 Company took over the front line and Nos.1 and 2 moved into support behind the road from O.13.d.9.8. to O.13.a.4.3.

This was to be the jumping off position for battalion in the attack on NOYELLES SUR SELLE at 09.45 hours on 13th October in the event of the attack by 7th battalion Argyll and Sutherland Highlanders on LIEU ST. AMAND being a success.

At 09.00 hours the 7th Argyll & Suth'd. Highrs. moved forward to attack the village of LIEU ST. AMAND but were held up by heavy machine gun fire from the village. In consequence of this No.4 Company on our left front did not advance. No.3 Company, however, found it possible to advance on MON. BLANCHE FARM and consolidated on either side of it being in touch with 152nd Infantry Brigade on their Right.

In the taking of this Farm No.3 Company met with intense enfilade machine gun fire from the village of LIEU ST. AMAND and the Wood 500 yards on their Right.

Before reaching the Farm a great proportion of the N.C.O's of the Company became casualties. The Company Commander and the Company Sergeant Major however collected the remainder of the Company and advanced again on the Farm and occupied it.

The line now taken up by the Battalion ran from O.8.a.85.20. to O.13.a.70.95. support companies remaining in original positions.

The Battalion was relieved on the night of the 14th/15th October, 1918 by the 6th Battalion Argyll & Sutherland Highlanders

During these operations the following casualties occurred:-

Officers. Killed 2. Wounded 2. N.Y.D. (Gas) 1.

O/Ranks. " 21. " 91. " " 6. Missing. 2.

(Sgd) L.D. HENDERSON, Major,
O.C. 4th Seaforth Highlanders.

17.25. hrs. 18/10/18.

1/4th Bn. SEAFORTH HIGHLANDERS.

HISTORY OF OPERATIONS 17/10/18 - 22/10/18.

Reference Map Sheet 51.A. 1/40,000 & Sketch maps attached.

17/19 Oct. Sketch Map. No. 1.

On 17th October the 154th Infantry Brigade moved from Divisional Reserve and took over a line from the 152nd Infantry Brigade. At 14.45 hours the 1/4th Seaforth Highlanders left THUN-ST.MARTIN and moved into Brigade Reserve at IWUY, relieving 6/7th Gordons. 1/4th Gordons ahd 1/7th Arg. & Suth. Highrs. were in line, the Gordons on Right and A. & S. H. on Left.

The companies took over the following positions, (See accompanying sketch map No.1):-

No.1 Co.	SUNKEN ROAD	N.36.d.
No.2 Co.	SUNKEN ROAD	O.31.c.
No.3 Co.		N.35.d.7.4.
No.4 Co.	SUNKEN ROAD	T.6.d.

19th Oct. Sketch Map No. 2.

The Battalion remained here till the evening of the 19th October, when it moved forward into line between the 1/4th Gordons and 1/7th A. & S. H., Nos. 1 and 2 companies lining the road running from O.14.b.15.95. to O.15.d.20.00., No.1 Company being on the Right, No.3 Company was in trenches at O.27.a. and No.4 Company dug in at O.29.d. (See sketch map No.2).

20th Oct. Sketch Map No. 3.

Between 01.00 hours and 02.00 hours on the 20th instant the battalion moved forward first to a position in field at O.10.a. where orders were issued for an advance in an Easterly direction from NOYELLES-SUR-SELLE (I.34). Companies accordingly moved forward and crossed the Selle by a pontoon bridge at I.29.c.15.05. and formed up on the East bank, on either side of the road running East from NOYELLES to MAISON ROUGE (I.35.a.), No.1 company being on the Right and No.3 Company on the Left; No.2 Company supporting No.1 Company and No.4 Company supporting No.3 Company (See sketch map No.3). At 04.45 hours companies were in position but came under fire of several machine guns when forming up. At 05.00 hours the advance commenced but could not be continued without heavy losses owing to machine gun fire. Companies therefore dug in slightly in advance of their assembly positions and endeavoured to locate machine guns which were troubling them. The advance was held up here until 10.15 hours when advance was again continued under a barrage. It however encountered heavy machine gun fire first from Sunken Road in I.36.b. and later from Railway Embankment in I.36.b. and d. and also in O.6.b. The Battalion was able, however, to reach the line of the Sunken Road in I.36.c. and O.6.a. with comparatively slight casualties, the advance being materially assisted on the right by a well aimed shot by a Sergeant of No.1 Company who at 500 yards range knocked out of action a machine gun, shooting the gunner clean through the heart. Nos. 1 and 3 companies dug in on the line of the Sunken Road in I.30.c and O.6.a., Nos 2 and 4 Coys digging in about 200 yards in rear (see sketch map No 3.) and waited for darkness to resume the advance. Companies were subjected to a considerable amount of harrassing machine gun fire during the day. Touch was obtained with 4th Gordon Hrs on right and 7th Arg. & Suth. Hrs on left. About 18.00 hours two platoons from the Support Coy. were sent forward to outpost positions East of the Railway at O.6.b.6.5 and I.36.d.6.6., machine gun fire having died down. During this phase of the operations Battalion H.Q. was in NOYELLES at I.34.d.7.7.

Sketch Map No.4

At 22.00 hours orders were issued for the advance to be resumed with Nos 2 and 4 Coys., the objectives being BOIS DE L' ENTREE and LE GRAND BOIS in J.32. These Companies accordingly sent forward two platoons each and reached their objective about midnight meeting with no opposition until the woods were reached when they came under machine gun fire and also heavy field gun fire, the latter being directed on the edge of the woods. The machine gun fire was

/eventually

eventually overcome but forward companies were compelled to dig in under heavy machine gun fire from the valley, though signs were not wanting that the enemy had only just vacated his positions here. Fire and food still warm were found in a house at J.31.d.8.7. The front companies now

21st Oct.

Sketch Map No. 4

brought forward their remaining platoons and dug in, No.2 Company from J.32.b.5.1. to P.2.b.6.6. and No.4 Company on East and North East edges of the BOIS DE L'ENTREE. Nos.1 and 3 companies moved forward in the early morning of the 21st and took up positions just behind the woods in support, No.1 Company in J.31.d. and P.2.a., and No.3 Company in J.32.a. Companies immediately on reaching their objectives were heavily shelled, direction being given to their artillery by means of VEREY lights which travelled a distance of fully 2000 yards. All through the day the enemy kept up a bombardment of the woods with 5.9's and gas but casualties were fortunately slight, though No.4 Company Commander Lieut. BESSANT was wounded in the afternoon.

These operations were undertaken in conjunction with the 4th Division on the Right, the 1/4th Gordons having been squeezed out and considerable difficulty occurred in getting into touch with this Division, contact not being established till 06.25 hours when the 4th Division established a post at P.2.b.7.4.

In the afternoon of the 21st instant word was received that MONCHAUX was occupied by 4th Division and that THIANT was occupied by the 1/7th Arg. & Suth. Highrs. The Battalion accordingly received instructions to push forward across the ECAILLON River and get contact with the enemy. Patrols were accordingly sent out at 17.00 hours but met with heavy M.G. fire from the village of MONCHAUX. At 20.00 hours on 21st instant No.4 Company extended their front Northwards about 700 yards in the direction of CLLE LOUVIERE (J.26.b.05.95), taking over this part of the line from 1/7th Arg. & Suth. Highrs.

22nd Oct.

Sketch Map No. 4.

Later in the day word was again received that MONCHAUX was occupied by the 4th Division, so about 02.00 hours on the 22nd instant the Battalion moved forward to occupy the high ground in J.29 and J.35. Patrols were sent out to secure bridgeheads but found all foot bridges to the North of MONCHAUX destroyed and ascertained from sound of movement and M.G. fire that the enemy was holding the East bank of the ECAILLON River in force. The patrol that was sent to MONCHAUX while still 20 yards from the River was fired on by two M.G's and lost four men out of six. The Battalion accordingly withdrew to its former positions.

At 09.30 a section of No.2 Company was sent forward to establish a post in Sunken Road J.33.b. but were unable to do so owing to M.G. fire. Two posts were however established here after dark at 17.00 hours. No.4 Company also pushed out a post to J.27.a.9.7.

The Battalion was relieved on the evening of the 22nd instant by the 1/6th Black Watch and went into reserve billets at DOUCHY.

From the resumption of the operations at 22.00 hours on the 20th instant until the Battalion was relieved, Battalion Headquarters was at LA MAISON ROUGE (I.36.a.4.2.). During all the operations communication between Battalion Headquarters and Company Headquarters was maintained by means of Lucas Lamps and this proved most efficient and satisfactory. It was found possible too to get the field cookers quite close to the companies and the hot meals which were thus able to be supplied to even the most forward posts helped to considerably counteract the adverse climatic conditions and to keep the spirits of the men up to a high level all through the operations.

(Sgd. L. D. HENDERSON, Major.
Commanding 1/4 Seaforth Highrs.

26th October, 1918.

2866

4th.Battn.Seaforth Highlanders.

Report on operations from the 26th. - 28th. October 1918.
on MOUNT HOUY.

Reference Map
MAING: 1/20,000.

PRELIMINARY. On the morning of the 27th.October 1918 4th.Seaforth Highrs. were concentrated in J.14.d. At 04.30 hours the Battalion ~~took over from~~ began to relieve the 6th.Black Watch and 6th.A. & S.Highrs. in FONTENELLE Sector.

At 16.00 hours on the 27th. orders were issued to the effect that 4th.Seaforth Highrs. would attack and capture MOUNT HOUY and gain final objective, which was to be from E.25.b.8.7. to E.26.a. 05.80. along enemy C.T. running through E.26.d. as far as E.26.d.4.6. thence swinging S.E. through CHEMIN VERT as far as K.3.c.4.8.

These orders were changed four hours later and final objective to be reached ran from E.25.b.8.7. to E.26.a.05.80 thence along enemy trench running through E.26.a. and E.27.c. to include the cemetery and cross roads of AULNOY in K.3.a. & b., a flank to be formed on the line of the FAMARS -AULNOY Road. A Coy. of 7th.A.& S.Hrs. in position in K.8.b. to be responsible for gaining this with the barrage from left of 6th.Seaforth Highrs. on right of our Brigade to house inclusive at K.3.c.70.95.which was to be the junction of 4th.Seaforth Highrs. In these subsequent orders there were two objectives - first and final. First objective ran from E.25.d.6.5. to E.27.a.4.8. thence in a straight line to K.8.b.7.1. First objective - Blue dotted line - final objective - Red dotted line.

ASSEMBLY. 4th.Seaforth Highlanders assembled for the attack with Nos. 1,2 & 4 Coys. in front (No.1 on the right ,No.2 in the centre and No. 4 on the left) with No. 3 Coy. in support. Front Coys. occupied a line running from K.1.b.0.4. - K.1.d.8.9. - K.1.d.7.0. - K.8.a.05.75. - K.8.c.5.9. No. 3 Coy. in support was in position immediately behind No. 1 Coy. A Coy. of 7th.Argylls was detailed to follow left front Coy. of 4th.Seaforth Highrs. This Coy. was to push on and endeavour to exploit along the Canal as far as E.20.central. If high ground above LA FARGETTE could be made it was to be occupied by this Coy. Two Coys. of Canadians to be at J.18. central and in the event of E.20 central being made by Coy. of 7th.Argylls, these two Coys. to push through and gain Southern outskirts of VALENCIENNES, and assist troops of Canadian Corps to cross to the Eastern side of the Canal.

The covering barrage was to advance 100 yards in 3 minutes. At zero plus 10 minutes the barrage to pause for 10 minutes on first objective. At zero plus 20 barrage to creep forward 100 yards in three minutes until final objective when it will pause for 15 minutes. Final protective barrage to cease at zero plus 90 minutes. The general direction of the attack to be North East.

OBJECTIVES OF COYS. Left front and centre Coys. to occupy and consolidate the final objective from E.25.b.8.7. to E.26.b.0.2. Centre Coy. from E.26.d. 10.75. to E.26.d.3.5. Right front Coy. to occupy and consolidate a line running through wood MOUNT HOUY from K.2.c.8.9. to K.8.b.3.9. Support Coy. to Leap frog right front Coy, two Platoons to capture and consolidate round cemetery and cross roads west of AULNOY gaining touch with 7th.A.& S.Hrs. at point K.3.c.7.9.. Remaining two Platoons to link up with centre Coy. on left

OBJECTIVES OF COYS. left/ and their own platoons on right N.W. of cross roads.

BATTLE. At 05.15 hours the barrage opened and the advance began, support Coy. advancing simultaneously with front Coys. and about 150 yards in rear.

Right Front. - On right front enemy S.O.S. barrage line was immediately in front of jumping off line, but Coy. was successful in getting through it before barrage fell. It came under heavy machine gun fire from wood . Enemy machine gun in position at K.2.d.1.4. gave some trouble but was rushed by a rifle section , the gun being captured and team killed. Two platoons worked round the right of the wood and two platoons round the left. The Quarry at S.W. edge of wood at K.2.c.6.5. was strongle held by the enemy. This was engaged by the two mobile field guns , which were in position behind FONTENELLE WOOD, 20 rounds b eing fired into it (See report from 2/Lieut.H.G.BEARD, R.F.A. attached) . Two sections worked round it and put one machine gun out of action , capturing 20 of the enemy who were taking cover in funk holes in the banks of the Quarry. This Coy. reached its objective and consolidated with 1 section in the wood at K.2.d.2.4. It accounted for 52 prisoners. The centre Coy. came under enemy barrage about 100 yards in front of jumping off line causing about 20 casualties. The first objective was reached at 05.40 hrs. about 40 prisoners were taken in the Quarry at K.2.a.55.35 and in surrounding shell hole posts. This Coy. was subjected to heavy machine gun fire throughout the Advance on first objective, the result being that the first wave was reduced to 16 O.R. on reaching blue dotted line. This wave consolidated on a line K.2.a.85.00. - K.2.a.5.4. At this stage touch was obtained on the right but not on the left. The second wave of Companies passed through at 0 5.50 hours, and in spite of heavy machine gun fire reached its objective at 06.15 hours, consolidating in enemy trench - Red dotted line , from E.26.d.3.7. to E.27.c.1,6.

Coy. was in touch with No. 3 Coy. on right but not with No. 4 Coy. on left. Only 12 O.R. of second wave got to the final objective.

The support Coy. leap frogged first objective, and two platoons swerved to the right towards cemetery, the other two platoons went forward to enemy trench in front and to the right of LE CHEMIN VERT. The two latter platoons reached their objectives and mopped up the trench to the right and to the left where they got in touch with centre Coys. During the process of mopping up one enemy Officer and 12 O.R. were killed, the remainder surrendering. The two platoons detailed to capture cross roads and cemetery got to within 200 yards of objective without a casualty . Here the Coy.Commander Lieut.W.R.Cullen was severely wounded in the thigh by a machine gun in the FAMARS - AULNOY Road . These two platoons ultimately gained their objective, but owing to the great number of small houses in the vicinity, which were strongly held by the enemy, and the fact that the 7th.A.& S.Highrs. had failed to get in touch with the right of the Coy. on the FAMARS - AULNOY Road , an immediate counter attack of the enemy succeeded in surrounding this party and it is surmised eventually captured them. The remaining two platoons of this Coy. were heavily engaged with the enemy on their objective and owing to the long distance between sections were unable to render any assistance

Left front Coy., although subjected to heavy machine gun fire from factories along Canal bank made good progress and captured and consolidated Blue dotted line to time. In doing so they captured 4 machine guns and their teams. Second wave of this Coy. leap frogged Blue line and made headway as far as Church in E.26.c. At this point heavy machine gun fire came from factories on left. The Coy.

~~XXXXXXXX~~
BATTLE.

Coy./ Commander immediately brought his Light Trench Mortar Gun into action. One direct hit was obtained on enemy machine gun and the team killed. These two sections were able to mop up factory buildings, capturing 4 machine guns and 2 teams - the other two teams having "skinned out". Another platoon pushed on towards buildings on left of Church. These buildings had a number of machine guns firing from them. Light trench morters again came into action, and Lieut.Hay in charge of gun put down a barrage with remaining bombs, thus enabling platoon to get forward. A lot of mopping up had to be done here and several prisoners were captured as well as 6 machine guns with their crews. The two platoons got in touch again and pushed on, but were compelled to consolidate about 200 yards from their objective. While consolidation was in progress platoons were subjected to heavy machine gun fire from LA TARGETTE . At this stage Coy.Commander moved forward one of his platoons from Blue line and called on two platoons of Coy. of 7th.A.& S.Hrs. to occupy position vacated in Blue line. Scouts were sent out to gain touch with Coy. on right, but this was found impossible owing to sniping and machine gun fire. This Coy. accounted for 65 prisoners and inflicted heavy casualties on the enemy.

At 08.15 hours the enemy put down a heavy barrage on final objective, and garrison holding out was in danger of being cut off owing to parties of the enemy dribbling in on them flank and rear. At the same time machine gun and rifle fire was directed on them from houses in LE CHEMIN VERT. These buildings could not be mopped up owing to strength of Coys. on gaining Blue dotted line. Le CHEMIN VERT represented 2 or 3 houses on the map, but Coys. found them to be a street of houses. The two remaining Officers of garrison decided to work along trench and gained touch with left front Coy. This was accomplished and a flank was put out - LE POIRIER Station to Crater in K.8.a. , thence to crater in K.8.b. being in touch with right front Coy. in occupation of a line running from K.8.c.6.4. to K.8.a.9.7. During the three hours following Zero , right front Coy., detailed to occupy Blue line running through MOUNT HOUY was continually harrassed by enemy machine guns concealed in wood, and when Coy.Commander found that front Coys. took up a line running to crater in K.8.c. he withdrew his Coy. and linked up with them on left - his new line now running to K.8.c.7.1. - K.8.a.9.7. Two more platoons from Coy. of 7 th.A.& S.Hrs. were brought forward to thicken the line from ~~XXXXXX~~ POIRIER Station to crater in K.8.c. In order to conform with the general line of defence taken up, left front Coy.Commander withdrew his two forward platoons to line E.25.a.4.6. - fork roads at POIRIER Station. Thus the line ran from E.25.d.4.6. - POIRIER Station - Crater in K. 8.a. - Crater in K. 8 C. - K.8.c.7.1. - K.8.a.9.7

A section of Vickers , in position at K.8.d.5.1, attacked and did very good work in accounting for several of the enemy.

At 16.00 hours the enemy artillery put down a very heavy barrage between railway line and wood after which a counter attack developed . Our Lewis Gun barrage prevented the enemy from leaving his assembly positions.

The Battalion was relieved by 6th.Argylls at 20.00 hrs. and moved back to CHATEAU DE PRES where it bivouacked for the night.

See attached page with reference to casualties and captures.

5th.November 1918.

Major,
Comdg.4th.Bn.Seaforth Hdgrs.

Casualties during operations
26th. october to 28th. October 1918.

OFFICERS.

Killed in Action.	2/Lt. W.Boardman D.C.M. Lieut. F.H.Ballantyne.
Wounded.	Lieut. W.R.Cullen. " G.Dickson. 2/Lt. J.A.Hogg.
Missing.	Lieut. J.A.Hermon. 2/Lt. C.J.Boyd.

OTHER RANKS.

Killed in action	7
Wounded	82
Missing	47.

Estimated number of prisoners captured	~~xxxx~~ 180.
Number of machine guns captured	21.

(All the M.Gs. were destroyed.)

465
6 sheets

Confidential.

War Diary

of

4th Battn. Seaforth Highrs.

Volume No. 50.

From. 1st November, 1918.
To - 30th November, 1918.

Army Form C. 2118.

Instructions regarding War Diaries and Intelligence Summaries are contained in F. S. Regs., Part II. and the Staff Manual respectively. Title pages will be prepared in manuscript.

WAR DIARY or INTELLIGENCE SUMMARY.

4th Battalion Seaforth Highlanders.

(Erase heading not required.)

Place	Date	Hour	Summary of Events and Information	Remarks and references to Appendices
Fbg. ST. ROCH	1/11/18		Cold morning but cleared up to fine day. Companies at the disposal of Company Commanders. Kit inspections under Coy. arrangements. Jw	
	2/11/18		Dull and cold day. Raining in the morning. Commanding Officer inspected Companies in the Recreation Hall. Companies engaged during the day in the clearing of the debris in front of billets. Jw	
	3/11/18		Dull day. Combined C of E and Presbyterian Service for whole Brigade, which was attended by Corps Commander. R.C. Service in church. Jw	
	4/11/18		Bright day. Companies re-organizing as per training scheme. Concert in conjunction with 'Balmorals' and Divisional Band. Jw	
	5/11/18		Dull morning and wet. Companies training in vicinity of billets. Specialist classes. All S.B.Rs in the Battalion tested in gas at Brigade H.Qrs. Jw	

(A9175) Wt W2358/P360 600,000 12/17 D. D. & L. Sch. 52a. Forms/C2118/15.

Army Form C. 2118.

Instructions regarding War Diaries and Intelligence Summaries are contained in F. S. Regs., Part II, and the Staff Manual respectively. Title pages will be prepared in manuscript.

WAR DIARY
or
~~INTELLIGENCE SUMMARY.~~
(Erase heading not required.)

Place	Date	Hour	Summary of Events and Information	Remarks and references to Appendices
FRE. ST. ROCH.	6/11/18		Dull day and raining. Companies training in open warfare on training area. Specialist Classes in afternoon. [initials]	
	7/11/18		Dull day and raining. Companies training in vicinity of billets. Specialist Classes and cleaning up of streets in front of billets. [initials]	
	8/11/18		Dull day and raining. Usual training. Lecture in Recreation room on Citizenship. Lt. Col. J. Cuthbert, D.S.O. rejoined the Battalion. [initials]	
	9/11/18		Fine day. Training in open warfare in the forenoon. Football match in the afternoon. [initials]	
	10/11/18		Bright day. Church services for all denominations. Draft of 4 Officers and 4 O.R. joined Battn. [initials]	

Army Form C. 2118.

Instructions regarding War Diaries and Intelligence Summaries are contained in F. S. Regs., Part II, and the Staff Manual respectively. Title pages will be prepared in manuscript.

WAR DIARY
or
~~INTELLIGENCE SUMMARY~~.
(Erase heading not required.)

Place	Date	Hour	Summary of Events and Information	Remarks and references to Appendices
FBG. ST ROCH	11/11/18		Dull and cold morning. Armistice between Germany and the Allies signed. Hostilities ceased at 11.00 hrs. Corps line running through MONS. General Holiday for the Division. Bath. Concert and whist drive in the evening. [initials]	
	12/11/18		Dull day but mild. Companies carry out usual training. Inspection of billets by G.O.C. [initials]	
	13/11/18		Frosty morning; bright day. Companies march to witness cross country race held by the Division. Our Battn. took fourth place. Concert and dance in the evening. [initials]	
	14/11/18		Fine day. Companies cleaning up and salvaging the training areas and vicinity of billets. [initials]	
	15/11/18		DITTO.	

(A9175) W: W2358/P360 600,000 12/17 D. D. & L. Sch. 52a. Forms/C2118/15.

Instructions regarding War Diaries and Intelligence Summaries are contained in F. S. Regs., Part II. and the Staff Manual respectively. Title pages will be prepared in manuscript.

WAR DIARY
or
~~INTELLIGENCE SUMMARY.~~
(Erase heading not required.)

Army Form C. 2118.

Place	Date	Hour	Summary of Events and Information	Remarks and references to Appendices
FBG. ST. ROCH	16/11/18		Fine day. Companies cleaning up and salvaging training areas & billets. [illegible]	
	17/11/18		Cold morning but fine day. Divine services for all denominations. [illegible]	
	18/11/18		Cold and dull day. Usual training and cleaning up of debris on Main Street. [illegible]	
	19/11/18		Fine day. Two Companies on training area and 2 Companies on range. [illegible]	
	20/11/18		Cold but fine day. Battalion route marching via FONTAINE. Concert in evening. [illegible]	
	21/11/18		Cold day. Coys. on training area. G.O.C. inspected the horses. Salvaging on training area. [illegible]	
	22/11/18		Cold but fine day. No. 4 Coy. on range. Remainder of Battn. on training and cleaning up roads. Lecture by senior Chaplain on "From War to Work". [illegible]	
	23/11/18		Cold day. Inspection of Battn. by C.O. Massed P.T. under P.T. instructors. [illegible]	

(A9175) Wt W2358/P360 600,000 12/17 D. D. & L. Sch. 52a. Forms/C2118/15.

Instructions regarding War Diaries and Intelligence Summaries are contained in F. S. Regs., Part II. and the Staff Manual respectively. Title pages will be prepared in manuscript.

WAR DIARY
or
~~INTELLIGENCE SUMMARY.~~
(Erase heading not required.)

Army Form C. 2118.

Place	Date	Hour	Summary of Events and Information	Remarks and references to Appendices
FBG. ST. ROCH.	24/11/18		Cold day. Divine services for all denominations.	
	25/11/18		Cold day. Inspection by B.G.C. cancelled. Coys. carrying on training.	
	26/11/18		Cold day. Two companies on range. Remainder of Battn. training on training area.	
	27/11/18		Cold day. Preliminary of Divl. Sports. Battalion march to Sports Ground.	
	28/11/18		Cold and raining. Training in billets. Lecture by C.O. in recreation room.	
	29/11/18		Cold and raining. Two Coys. on the range. Two Coys. route marching.	
	30/11/18		Cold day. Final of Divisional Sports. Bn. marched to sports area. Officers' dinner to celebrate St. Andrew's day.	
			[signature], Lt. Col., Commanding, 4th Bn. Seaforth Highrs.	

(A9175) Wt W2358/P363 600,000 12/17 D. D. & L. Sch. 52a. Forms/C2118/15.

154th Infantry Brigade.

Reference B. 280.

Up to date no medium T.M. have been attached to this Unit but it is considered that the Light T.M. is quite heavy enough for the posts encountered or for following up a rear guard in open warfare.

(a). A pouch equipment after the pattern of that used for L.G. Drums would be useful for carrying a small amount of ammunition with the gun.

(b). A half limber of ammunition or a Pack mule should be kept close up in rear of the Companies to which the section or half section of T.M.B. is attached. If circumstances permit the limber or pack mule can be brought up or the men carrying the pouch equipment can go back to the limber or pack mule for ammunition.

(c). The sections of T.M.B. should be allotted to Companies by Battn. Commanders according to ground over which they are attacking. They were found very valuable in buildings and woods and affected the morale of the enemy considerably as well as causing a number of casualties.

(d). The method of liasion should be direct between the Officer or N.C.O. commanding the section and the Company or Platoon Officer. It is essentially a weapon of opportunity and must be brought into action immediately the section scouts have located the enemy post.

(e). In the operations at MONT HUOY on the 28th October, 1918 a section of a T.M.B. was operating with the Company Commander of the left Company attacking through a network of Factory Buildings' houses. A gun was brought into action immediately any opposition was encountered and although it was only possible to carry 12 Rds. of ammunition the following results were achieved:-

1. A direct hit on an enemy M.G. Post.
2. In some cases enemy surrendered or retired as soon as the T.M. came into action.
3. By putting a few rounds about an enemy M.G. post the enemy kept under cover and the Infantry were enabled to work up close enough to rush the Post.

[signature]

Major,

5 .11.1918. Commanding, 4th Bn. Seaforth Highldrs.

(Confidential.)

War Diary

of

4th. Battn. Seaforth Highrs.

Volume 51

from 1st. December 1918

to 31st December 1918.

4th Bn. Seaforth Highlanders

Instructions regarding War Diaries and Intelligence Summaries are contained in F. S. Regs., Part II. and the Staff Manual respectively. Title pages will be prepared in manuscript.

WAR DIARY
or
INTELLIGENCE SUMMARY.
(*Erase heading not required.*)

Army Form C. 2118.

Place	Date	Hour	Summary of Events and Information	Remarks and references to Appendices
ESCAUDOEUVRES	1/12/18		Cold day. Divine Service for all denominations. Lecture by Educational Officer on "The New Franchise" 2 Lt. G.R. Coutts joined the Battn.	
	2/12/18		Battn. parade. Training of drafts in musketry etc.	
	3/12/18		Nos. 1 & 2 Coys. on the range and Nos 3 & 4 Coys. on short route marches. Lecture by Educational Officer.	
	4/12/18		Nos. 2 & 4 Coys. carried out training. No 3 Coy. Lewis Gunnery & Musketry, No 1 Coy. at the Baths.	
	5/12/18		Coys. on salvage work. Commencement of classes under the Army Education scheme. H.Q. Coy. at baths.	
	6/12/18		No. 3 & 4 Coys. on Rifle range. Nos. 1 & 2 Coys. carried out training. The Commanding Officer inspected the recently arrived Drafts.	
	7/12/18		Battn. carried out training behind Battn. H.Q. Football match between right half Battn. & 1st (H) Field Ambulance.	
	8/12/18		Sunday. Good day. Church parades. Football match between 4th Seaforths (left half) and 7th Argylls (left half.)	
	9/12/18		Good day. Coys. carried out training on Battn. parade ground. Rugby match in afternoon.	

(A6175) Wt W2358/P360 600,000 12/17 D. D. & L. Sch. 52a. Forms/C2118/15.

Instructions regarding War Diaries and Intelligence Summaries are contained in F. S. Regs., Part II. and the Staff Manual respectively. Title pages will be prepared in manuscript.

WAR DIARY
or
INTELLIGENCE SUMMARY.
(Erase heading not required.)

Army Form C. 2118.

Place	Date	Hour	Summary of Events and Information	Remarks and references to Appendices
ESCAUDOEUVRES	10/12/18		Wet day. Bad shots of each Coy. fired on Range. Coys. training near billets.	
	11/12/18		Wet day. Route march cancelled. Training carried on in billets.	
	12/12/18		Wet day. Training as on previous day.	
	13/12/18		Good day. Shooting competition on range.	
	14/12/18		Good day. Usual Company training.	
	15/12/18		Do. Sunday. Divine Services for all denominations.	
	16/12/18		Wet day. Nos 1 & 2 Coys. carried out training. Nos 3 & 4 Coys at the Baths.	
	17/12/18		Good day. Nos. 1 & 2 Coys. fired on range and Nos 3 & 4 Coys. drill & training.	
	18/12/18		Wet day. Intended route march to MARCOING cancelled. Indoor training by Coys.	
	19/12/18		Wet day. Usual training, drill etc.	
	20/12/18		Good day but very cold. Coys. carried out training on Battn. parade ground.	
	21/12/18		Good day but cold. Do Do.	
	22/12/18		Dull day & cold. Divine Services for all denominations.	
	23/12/18		Battn. carried out salvage work clearing shells, equipment etc & taking them to Dump at IWUY. Dull boisterous day.	
	24/12/18		Good day but very cold. Coys. on salvage work. Football match between 4th Seaforths & 7th Argylls	

(A6175) Wt W2358/P364 600,000 12/17 D. D. & L. Sch. 52a. Forms/C2118/15.

Army Form C. 2118.

WAR DIARY
or
INTELLIGENCE SUMMARY.
(*Erase heading not required.*)

Instructions regarding War Diaries and Intelligence Summaries are contained in F. S. Regs., Part II. and the Staff Manual respectively. Title pages will be prepared in manuscript.

Place	Date	Hour	Summary of Events and Information	Remarks and references to Appendices
ESCAUDOEUVRES	25/12/18		Christmas day. General holiday in the Army. Each Coy. had a Christmas dinner & concert. Battn. concert party gave an entertainment in the evening. Good day but cold.	
	26/12/18		Boxing day. Battn. carried out Salvage work. Good weather.	
	27/12/18		Good day but very cold. Cross country run at 10.30 hrs.	
	28/12/18		Wet day. Cross country race in the morning.	
	29/12/18		Wet day. Sunday. Divine Service.	
	30/12/18		Dull day. Battn. carried out Salvage work. Football match, 4th Seaforths versus 4th Gordons.	
	31/12/18		Wet day. Holiday for the Battn. Cross country Divisional race at THUN LEVECQUE. This Battn. took second place.	

(A9175) Wt W2358/P360 600,000 12/17 D. D. & L. Sch. 52a. Forms/C2118/15.

Headquarters
154th Infantry Bde.

Confidential

Aof O

War Diary

of

4th Bn. Seaforth Hrs.

Vol. 52

From January 1st 1919 to January 31st 1919

[signature]
Major
Comdg. 4th Bn. Seaforth Hrs.

1 · 2 · 19

4th Bn. Seaforth Highlanders Vol. 52.

Instructions regarding War Diaries and Intelligence Summaries are contained in F. S. Regs., Part II. and the Staff Manual respectively. Title pages will be prepared in manuscript.

WAR DIARY
or
INTELLIGENCE SUMMARY.
(*Erase heading not required.*)

Army Form C. 2118.

Place	Date	Hour	Summary of Events and Information	Remarks and references to Appendices
St. Roch	1/1/19		Good day but cold. Holiday for Battn. it being New Years Day.	
	2/1/19		Good day ~~but~~ very cold. Battn. carry out salvage work with the exception of H.Q. Coy and Transport who have baths.	
	3/1/19		Good day. Part of Battn on baths and remainder on salvage work.	
	4/1/19		Good day but very cold. Recognised Battn holiday. Cross country race.	
	5/1/19		Sunday – Wet day. Divine Service for all denominations. Pres. 11.30 hrs. C. of E. 09.00 hrs. R.C. 10.00 hrs.	
	6/1/19		Good day. No 3 Coy fire on range while remainder of Battn carry on salvage work. Inspection of billets by Commanding Officer.	
	7/1/19		Good day. No 4 Coy fire on range while remainder of Battn carry on salvage work.	
	8/1/19		Good day. Battn on salvage work and baths. Inspection of rifles & kits by O.C. Companies. Football match. 4th Seaforths v 8th Bn. Worcesters.	
	9/1/19		Wet day. Battn ~~Mass parade at [illegible]~~ Baths for those who did not have them the previous day. Football match 4th Seaforths (R.H.) v 4th Gordons (L.H.)	

(A9175) Wt W2358/P360 600,000 12/17 D. D. & L. Sch. 52a. Forms/C2118/15.

4th Bn. Seaforth Hrs.

Instructions regarding War Diaries and Intelligence Summaries are contained in F. S. Regs., Part II. and the Staff Manual respectively. Title pages will be prepared in manuscript.

WAR DIARY
or
INTELLIGENCE SUMMARY.
(Erase heading not required.)

Army Form C. 2118.

Place	Date	Hour	Summary of Events and Information	Remarks and references to Appendices
St Roch.	10/1/19		Good day but very cold. Marching order inspection by O.C. Coys. After inspection Coys carry out training and clean up billets & vicinity.	T.F.
	11/1/19		Good day. Battn. leave St Roch 08·30 hrs in motor busses and arrive in Houdeng-Aimeries (Belgium) about 15·30 hrs. Battn. are billeted with the civilians who show great hospitality to the men.	T.F.
Houdeng Aimeries	12/1/19		Good day. Sunday – no church parade for Battn.	T.F.
	13/1/19		Good day. The following programme of training was carried out:- Inspection of Coys (walking out dress), Saluting drill, Coy. route marches, route chosen by Coy Commanders.	T.F.
	14/1/19		Good day. Battn. mass parade in marching order. Football match 4th Seaforths (L.H.) v 7th Argylls (L.H.) at La Louvière.	T.F.
	15/1/19		Wet day. Coys parade under Coy arrangements with the exception of men for sports. Medical inspection of men in billets.	T.F.
	16/1/19		Good day. Battn. have baths at St. Joseph's School.	T.F.
	17/1/19		Good day but very cold. Battn parade full marching order with the exception of men for sports.	T.F.

(A9175) Wt W2358/P360 600,000 12/17 D. D. & L. Sch. 52a. Forms/C2118/15.

4th Bn. Seaforth Hrs.

Instructions regarding War Diaries and Intelligence Summaries are contained in F. S. Regs., Part II. and the Staff Manual respectively. Title pages will be prepared in manuscript.

WAR DIARY
or
INTELLIGENCE SUMMARY.
(*Erase heading not required.*)

Army Form C. 2118.

Place	Date	Hour	Summary of Events and Information	Remarks and references to Appendices
Houdeng-Aimeries	18/1/19		Good day. Recognised Battn. holiday. Football match 4th Seaforths v 6/7th Gordons.	
	19/1/19		Sunday. Good day. Divine Service for all denominations i.e. 11.00 hrs C of E 11.30 hrs. R.C. 09.30 hrs.	
	20/1/19		Good day. Training carried out according to programme. Inter-Coy Rugby Football match on Battn. Ground.	
	21/1/19		Good day. Training carried out according to programme.	
	22/1/19		Good day but very cold. Battn. have baths at St. Joseph's School.	
	23/1/19		Good day but very cold. Training carried out according to programme.	
	24/1/19		Good day but very cold. Training carried out according to programme. Battn. Concert given by Battn. Concert Party in Houdeng-Goegnies	
	25/1/19		Good day but very cold. Recognised Battn. holiday.	
	26/1/19		Very cold and a good fall of snow. Divine Service for all denominations, i.e. 10.00 hrs C of E 11.00 hrs R.C. 09.30 hrs.	
	27/1/19		Good day but very cold. Training carried out according to programme.	

(A9175) Wt W2358/P360 600,000 12/17 D. D. & L. Sch. 52a. Forms/C2118/15.

4th Seaforth Hrs.

Instructions regarding War Diaries and Intelligence Summaries are contained in F. S. Regs., Part II, and the Staff Manual respectively. Title pages will be prepared in manuscript.

Army Form C. 2118.

WAR DIARY
or
INTELLIGENCE SUMMARY.
(Erase heading not required.)

Place	Date	Hour	Summary of Events and Information	Remarks and references to Appendices
Houdeng-Aimeries	28/1/19		Good day but very cold. Battn. have baths at St Joseph's School, Houdeng-Goegnies. Prince of Wales visits Houdeng-Aimeries.	[initials]
	29/1/19		Good day. No. 1 Coy. fire on range at Fosse, while remainder of Battn. carry out training according to programme.	[initials]
	30/1/19		Good day. Training carried out according to programme.	[initials]
	31/1/19		Good day. Training carried out according to programme until 10.30 hrs, when Coys. will have short Cross Country route marches.	[initials]

K.D. Henderson
Major
1.2.19. Comdg. 4th Bn. Seaforth Hrs.

(A9175) Wt W2358/P363 600,000 12/17 D. D. & L. Sch. 52a. Forms/C2118/15.

Original

Confidential

War Diary

of

1/4th Seaforth Highlanders

Vol 53.

From 1st Feb 1919 To 28th Feb 1919.

(6392) Wt. W6192/P875 1,500,000 4/18 McA & W Ltd (E 2815) Forms W3091/4. Army Form W.3091.

Cover for Documents.

Nature of Enclosures.

Notes, or Letters written.

4th Bn Seaforth Hrs.

Vol 53

Instructions regarding War Diaries and Intelligence Summaries are contained in F. S. Regs., Part II. and the Staff Manual respectively. Title pages will be prepared in manuscript.

WAR DIARY or ~~INTELLIGENCE~~ SUMMARY.

(Erase heading not required.)

Army Form C. 2118.

Place	Date	Hour	Summary of Events and Information	Remarks and references to Appendices
1919 HOUDENG-GOEGNIES.				
	1/2/19		Good day Recognised Battalion Holiday. JMc	
	2/2/19		Good day Divine service for all denominations, presbyterian 1100 hrs C of E. 10 00 hours. R.C. 09 30 hrs JMc	
	3/2/19		Good day but cold, Battalion had baths at St Josephs School HOUDENG-GOEGNIES. JMc	
	4/2/19		Good day, Training carried out according to programme issued. JMc	
	5/2/19		Good day Training carried out according to programme. No 2 Coy fired on the range at FOSSE. JMc	
	6/2/19		Heavy fall of snow. Battalion carried out a short route march. JMc	
	7/2/19		Good day. Companies at disposal of Coy Commanders according to programme JMc	
	8/2/19		Muster parade on Battalion parade ground of all ranks who volunteer or are liable for service with Armies of Occupation. JMc	
	9/2/19		No divine services. Muster parade same as yesterday. JMc	

(A9175) Wt W2358/P360 600,000 12/17 D. D. & L. Sch. 52a. Forms/C2118/15.

Instructions regarding War Diaries and Intelligence Summaries are contained in F. S. Regs., Part II. and the Staff Manual respectively. Title pages will be prepared in manuscript.

WAR DIARY
or
~~INTELLIGENCE SUMMARY.~~ 4th Bn Seaforth Hrs.

(Erase heading not required.)

Army Form C. 2118.

Place	Date	Hour	Summary of Events and Information	Remarks and references to Appendices
HOUDENG-GOEGNIES	10/2/19		Training according to programme and education classes. JM	
	11/2/19		Battalion had baths to-day at St. Josephs School, HOUDENG-GOEGNIES JM	
	12/2/19		Companies at disposal of Coy Commanders, according to programme issued. JM	
	13/2/19		Good day Same as yesterday. JM	
	14/2/19		Good day Training according to programme. JM	
	15/2/19		Good day. Recognised battalion holiday. JM	
	16/2/19		Divine service for all denominations, presbyterians 10.00 hours, R.C. 09.30 hrs. C. of E. 1100 hours. JM	
	17/2/19		Good day Training carried out according to programme. JM	
	18/2/19		Good day Same as yesterday. JM	
	19/2/19		Baths at St. Josephs School HOUDENG-GOEGNIES for the battalion. JM	
	20/2/19		Muster parade of battalion, after which companies carried out training under Coy arrangements. JM	
	21/2/19		Good day. All N.C.O's parade under Adjt. on battalion parade ground. JM	
	22/2/19		Good day. Recognised battalion holiday. JM	

(A9175) Wt W2358/P360 600,000 12/17 D. D. & L. Sch. 52a. Forms/C2118/15.

Instructions regarding War Diaries and Intelligence Summaries are contained in F. S. Regs., Part II. and the Staff Manual respectively. Title pages will be prepared in manuscript.

Army Form C. 2118.

WAR DIARY
or
~~INTELLIGENCE SUMMARY~~.

(Erase heading not required.)

4th Bn. Seaforth Hrs.

Place	Date	Hour	Summary of Events and Information	Remarks and references to Appendices
HOUDENG GOEGNIES	23/2/19		Battalion stand-by prepared to move to 2nd Army. No divine service	
	24/2/19		Same as yesterday. No parades.	
	25/2/19		Same as yesterday.	
	26/2/19		Battalion proceeded to join 62nd Division, (Armies of Occupation) entraining at MANAGE.	
	27/2/19		The day was spent in travelling	
	28/2/19		Battalion arrived at MECKERNICH. and proceeded on foot to occupy billets in EMBKEN and GINNICK, being attached to 187 Infantry Bde, 62nd Division.	

[illegible signature]
Lieut-Col.
Commanding 4th Bn. Seaforth Hrs.

(A9175) Wt W2358/P360 600,000 12/17 D. D. & L. Sch. 52a. Forms/C2118/15.

www.ingramcontent.com/pod-product-compliance
Lightning Source LLC
Chambersburg PA
CBHW081438160426
43193CB00013B/2321